Go TEAM!
Dear Bria
Thank you that you do!
— Judy

GO TEAM!

The Power of Team In Training

Dear Brian —
Thanks so much for all you do for LLS + TNT!
— Dan

Judy Mansisidor
Dan McCann

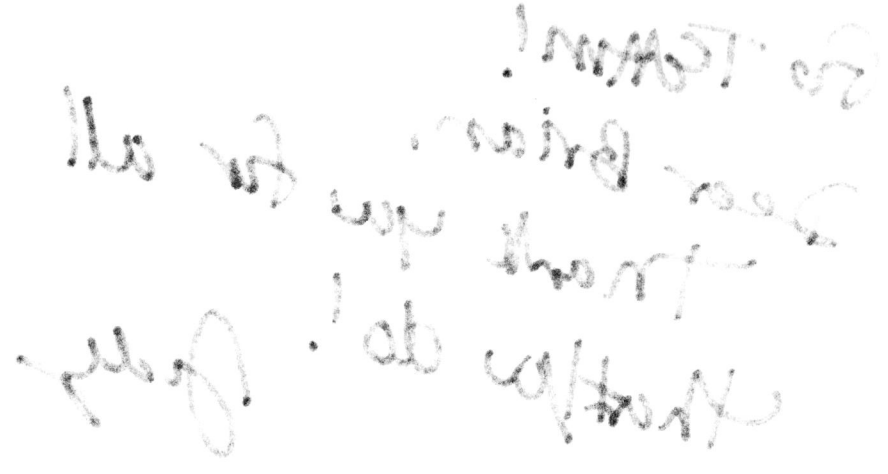

Copyright © 2015 Go Team LLC
All rights reserved.

ISBN: 1505437954
ISBN 13: 9781505437959

Cover photos courtesy of:
Art Herman
Viviana Maldonado
Kelly McCann
Scott & Lisa McCoid
Peggy Kreuger

Table of Contents

Foreword ix

Chapter 1: Iron Sharpens Iron 1

Chapter 2: The Information Meeting 5
    Athlete Reflections: "How Can I Not?" –
    Jen Kwasny, TNT athlete 9
    Athlete's Journey: Shambra L. Clifford's Story – Part I 11
    Athlete's Journey: Julie Petersen's Story – Part I 11
    Athlete Journey: Katie Sullivan Poppert's Story – Part I 14
    Team In Training Spotlight: The Genesis of TNT –
    The Cleland Story 15
    The Battle against Cancer: On the Front Lines 22

Chapter 3: Why We Team 25
    Athlete Reflections: "Little Did I Know How Much It Would
    Help Me too" – Kelly McCann, TNT run coach/athlete 27
    Athlete Reflections: "Who Can Say No to
    Their Big Sister?" – Mike McAtee, TNT athlete 27
    Athlete Reflections: "Only If I Run It for
    Team In Training!" – Tasha Hunt, TNT athlete 32
    Team In Training Spotlight: Running through Grief –
    The Lucy Duffy Story 33
    The Battle against Cancer: On the Front Lines 36

Chapter 4: First Miles 40
    Athlete's Journey: Katie Sullivan Poppert's Story – Part II ... 44
    Athlete Reflections: "We Never Train Alone." –
    Phil Ham, TNT athlete 46
    The Battle against Cancer: On the Front lines............... 48

Chapter 5: Group Training... 52
    Athlete's Journey: Art Herman's Story – Part I 54
    Athlete's Journey: Shambra L. Clifford's Story – Part II 56
    Athlete Reflections: "I Could Not Have Been More Wrong." –
    Mackenzie Raber, TNT athlete 57
    Athlete Reflections: "Because I Can" –
    Angie Dougherty, TNT athlete/mentor.......................... 59
    Team In Training Spotlight: Any Given Saturday –
    A Coaches' Perspective on Group Training 62

Chapter 6: Meeting the Honored Hero 66
    A Survivor's Story: Heartbreak and Triumph:
    A Pep Talk to the Team – Ashley True, TNT honored
    teammate... 69
    Honored Heroes: For My Mother Maria –
    Laura Korkowski, TNT athlete 72
    Honored Heroes: For My Husband Mike –
    Judy Mansisidor, TNT athlete 75
    Honored Heroes: For My Husband, Mauri –
    Mary Ellen Hellerstedt, TNT athlete...........................76
    A Survivor's Story: The Power to Persevere –
    Elizabeth Kerans, TNT honored teammate.....................78
    Team In Training Spotlight: "Cancer Brought
    Me Closer to God" – Judy Gillette, a survivor's story........... 80
    The Battle against Cancer: On the Front Lines 82

Chapter 7: Fundraising 101: The Money & the Mission............. 86
    Athlete Reflections: A Giver Who Kept on Giving –
    Jenna Hardy, TNT athlete 89

Athlete's Journey: Katie Sullivan Poppert's Story – Part III 91
Team In Training Spotlight: A Fundraising Phenomenon! – The Team WillyK Story: Part I 93

Chapter 8: Heart of the Season 101
  Athlete Reflections: "It Was a Headache, Not Cancer." -- Shannon Snow, TNT athlete. 104
  Athlete's Journey: Katie Sullivan Poppert's Story – Part IV 107
  Athlete Reflections: "20 Miles Is Different from Everything." – Meghan Fitzpatrick, TNT athlete. 111
  Athlete Reflections: "A Milestone for Sure" – Scott J. McCoid, TNT athlete. 112
  Team In Training Spotlight: A Fundraising Phenomenon! – The Team WillyK Story: Part II 113
  The Battle against Cancer: On the Front Lines 117

Chapter 9: Heartbreak & Hope 119
  Athlete Reflections: "Go Running. That's Your Job." – A.P. Beemer, TNT athlete 123
  The Battle against Cancer: On the Front Lines 125
  Athlete Reflections: "My Teammates Were There for Me." – Claudia Garcia, TNT athlete. 127
  The Battle against Cancer: On the Front Lines 129

Chapter 9: Heartbreak & Hope 133
  Athlete Reflections: "Today Was about Knowing that I Can Finish 26.2." – Shannon Snow, TNT athlete. 135
  Miracle Moment: My Angel Plays Bagpipes – Kelly McCann, TNT coach/athlete. 137
  Miracle Moment: Pennies from Heaven – Kristi Kempkes, TNT athlete. 140
  Miracle Moment: A Short Rest – and a Little Prayerful Intervention – Andi Mucklow, TNT athlete. 141

Team In Training Spotlight: "You Just Have to Keep Fighting" – The David Gong Story..................142
The Battle against Cancer: On the Front Lines............150

Chapter 10: Event Weekend..................................161
    Athlete's Journey: Shambra L. Clifford's Story – Part III.....163
    Athlete's Journey: Art Herman's Story – Part II............165
    Athlete's Journey: Katie Sullivan Poppert's Story – Part IV..................167
    The Battle against Cancer: On the Front Lines............170

Chapter 11: On the Course...................................172
    Athlete Reflections: "What a Journey This Has Been!" – Scott J. McCoid, TNT athlete.............176
    Athlete Reflections: Faith, God and Rock-n-Roll – Kara M. Lau, TNT athlete................................177
    Athlete Reflections: "I Have Never Been So Humbled." – Carol Obenauer, TNT athlete................................181
    Athlete's Journey: Julie Petersen's Story – Part II..........182
    Athlete's Journey: Art Herman's Story – Part III...........184
    Athlete's Journey: Katie Sullivan Poppert's Story – Part V....185
    Team In Training Spotlight: "Never Judge..." – Judy Mansisdor, a runner's story........................189
    The Battle against Cancer: On the Front Lines............191

Chapter 12: Crossing the Finish line 193
    Athlete Reflections: A TNT Member for Life – Mackenzie Raber, TNT athlete................................195
    Athlete's Journey: Katie Sullivan Poppert's Story – Part VI..................................197
    Athlete Reflections: Acting on a Dream Ann Herzinger, TNT athlete................................199
    Athlete Reflections: "Team In Training Is a Celebration." -- Angie Crawford, TNT athlete............................202

Team In Training Spotlight: The Genesis of TNT –
The Cleland Story – Part II................................. **205**

Chapter 13: Someday **207**

Foreword

GO TEAM! THE POWER OF TEAM IN TRAINING

Go Team!

If you've been at any endurance event recently, chances are you've heard this shouted by anyone and everyone wearing a purple jersey – "Go Team!"

What is this "Go Team" about? What is conveyed and shared in that short burst among teammates and their supporters?

To fully understand it, you have to understand Greek. Don't panic – it is just one word: dunamis, the Greek word for power. According to Strong's Concordance, word 1411, dunamis is defined as: *Inherent power, power residing in a thing by virtue of its nature, or which a person or thing exerts and puts forth.*

Dunamis is further defined as five very specific exertions:
1. **A power for performing miracles**
2. **The moral power and excellence of the soul**
3. **The power and influence which belongs to riches and wealth**
4. **The power and resources arising from numbers**
5. **The power consisting or resting in armies, forces or angels**

As you read these stories and correspondence from Team In Training (TNT) athletes and coaches, patients, researchers and family members – all fronts of the cancer battle – you will see the power of TNT shine in each of those exertions:

1. **As a power for performing miracles**

FDA approved in 1997, the drug Rituximab represents a miraculous breakthrough in treating lymphomas. While doctors still do not fully understand how the drug works, the research, funded in part by Team In Training athletes, has given rise to many new strategies for battling other cancers.

2. **As the moral power and excellence of the soul**

In the many stories of patients and loved ones fighting together for life, battles are won and lost – and souls are truly revealed – in critical situations. Athletes repeatedly demonstrate that they have the heart to rise above extremely challenging and seemingly impossible obstacles to join in the battles against blood cancers.

3. **As the power and influence which belongs to riches and wealth**

In 2013, the Leukemia & Lymphoma Society (LLS) invested $73.8 million in research: $8.4 million in myelodysplastic syndromes/**myeloproliferative** diseases (MDS/MPD), $9.8 million in myeloma, $20.4 million in lymphoma and $35.2 million in leukemia.[1]

4. **As the power and resources arising from numbers**

Team In Training athletes participate in over 200 endurance events per year. A typical TNT athlete will cover approximately 550 miles or more to prepare for one marathon!

5. **As the power consisting or resting in armies, forces or angels.**

The ranks of Team In Training "angels" – the athletes alone – have grown to over 600,000 since TNT's inception in 1988. [2] There is always room for one more teammate – *you*!

---

[1] www.lls.org/aboutlls/financialinformation/annualreports
[2] http://www.lls.org/content/nationalcontent/pdf/LLS_2013_AR.pdf

Now that you have an understanding of the power of TNT, we challenge you to read these blood cancer battle and survival stories and allow them to seep into your own heart and soul.

Don't be surprised if you find yourself shouting "GO TEAM!" Then, it will hit you – that YOU have it in you to fight bravely against myeloma, leukemia, lymphoma and other related cancers; that you have it in you to harness that "GO TEAM" power, that dunamis – and complete your first (or next) endurance event in purple as well!

GO TEAM!
– **Judy Mansisidor**, TNT Alum
– **Dan McCann**, TNT Alum & Marathon Coach,
Nebraska Chapter, TNT Flex

The views and opinions expressed in this book are those of the authors/editors, contributors and interview subjects. They do not necessarily represent the views and opinions of, and should not be attributed to, the Leukemia & Lymphoma Society or its Team In Training program.

It was all coming together for Bruce and Izzi Cleland – a beautiful young family, success in the futures brokerage business...

Then in October 1985, it all started coming apart.

Bruce awoke one morning to discover that Rudolf Wolff, his London-based employer since 1973, had suffered massive bad debt: the capital base of the entire metal brokerage giant – and the equity interest he had built up in his New York office – was almost entirely wiped out.

It was up to him, in early 1986, to negotiate the sale of the very international division he was running. Then, on March 21st of that year, right in the middle of this onerous transaction, his daughter, Georgia, was diagnosed with cancer...

...A cancer diagnosis coupled with a father's determined love...

That's really how it all began.

Since 1988, a collective "Team" of more 600,000 runners, walkers, triathletes, cyclists and hikers has embraced what Bruce Cleland created, raising more than $1.4 billion dollars to alleviate – and ultimately eliminate – the cancer-driven suffering of others.

This is not a book about how to train for endurance events.

This is a book about why we train for endurance events.

One

Iron Sharpens Iron

I am a Team In Training coach – and there are 2,300 others across the country just like me. I, like them, have seen "ordinary" human beings push themselves to the breaking point – and beyond. Voluntarily. These men and women – these Team In Training (TNT) athletes – are my inspiration. My heroes…

Terry was struggling when I came upon him – mile 22 of the Chicago Marathon, October 7, 2012. Every step was a battle, an exercise in excruciating pain.

"What's going on, Terry?" I asked, glancing at the name emblazoned across the front of his purple Team In Training jersey, nodding to the younger man he was walking with.

"My knees," he replied. "They feel like they're about to explode, like a guitar string that's about to pop."

It was very late in the game, afternoon temperatures were starting to revert back to chilly morning lows. (To ward off the cool, Terry had claimed a pair of sweatpants someone ditched along the course. Jungle rules.) The original field of about 40,000 had dwindled to a few hundred. Maybe less. Race volunteers were starting to dismantle the course.

"How about we get you to the medical tent," I said, "get you checked out."

He kept moving forward. Slowly. He acknowledged the pain – a 9.5 on his scale – but wasn't miserable about it.

"Is this your son?" I asked, referring to his course support.

"No," Terry corrected, "this is my nephew, David."

"Hey David," I said as I shifted my running pack from my backside to the front and fished out my cell phone. "I'm going to see if we can get you a ride to the medical tent, alright?"

Terry pushed on. Step by painful step. A support vehicle, I learned, would be waiting at 33rd & State St., about a-quarter-mile ahead. We walked on. Terry's phone rang. His son was checking in, his voice the very fuel Terry needed at that very moment – reassurance and re-focus. That, along with a few squat-type stretches and a change of walking surface (from concrete to a more forgiving asphalt), offered a slight reprieve from the misery.

With 33rd & State St. now just ahead, we needed to make a decision. Forgo the support vehicle here, and there would not be another opportunity. We'd have to call a cab if things took a turn for the worse. I nudged Terry to take the ride. He felt, at that point, like he could push on. And he did, fighting for every step.

While volunteers and workers continued to dismantle the massive endeavor, we soldiered on, maneuvering around brooms and dump trucks, moving to the sidewalk, stopping for traffic lights. A few other walkers straggled. Terry, amidst his pain, smiled and asked another walker, "Wanna race?"

"We're going to win next year," the woman replied.

Life can be very complicated at times. We are bombarded with decisions – *if this then that* – and a myriad of choices we have to make. On the course, it is very simple: finish or don't finish. Terry made his choice, and now our only option was to keep moving forward. Period. Wonderfully, painfully black and white.

As we churned toward mile 24, I asked, "What brought you to the Team?" – a common question on the course.

Terry, it turns out, was racing for his brother – David's father – who had passed away from leukemia three years prior.

Cancer.

Terry recalled the intense pain his brother endured and how, even while wracked with that pain, he still found the strength to preach the Gospel to his nurse.

"David is strong like his father," Terry said of his nephew, another child left behind. Then, wracked with his own physical pain, Terry was, himself, moved to quote the Gospel: "As iron sharpens iron, so one man sharpens another." (Proverbs 27:17)

"You two sharpen me," he said.

"I'm honored" was all I could think to reply – and then I shared one of my favorite verses, Roman 5:3-4: "We rejoice in our sufferings, knowing that suffering produces endurance, and endurance produces character, and character produces hope." For me, there is no better encapsulation of the Team In Training experience. TNT athletes produce hope through their suffering – physical suffering and the mental strain that comes from venturing beyond one's comfort zone. Is it suffering like a cancer patient suffers? Absolutely not. But it is suffering none-the-less – the sacrificing of one's body, one's very self, to alleviate the suffering of others. There is a name for people like that: heroes.

Terry was my hero that day in Chicago. He stood up to the intense pain – and kept moving forward. Step-by-agonizing-step. And, he finished the race with his nephew at his side. I left the two at mile 26 with hugs and words of admiration. The last .2 was theirs to share – no third wheel needed.

Days after the race, I was blessed to receive an email from Terry that read, "God used you to encourage and bless me when you shared Romans 5:3-4 with David and me right when I needed it!"

Terry was one of the last people on the course that day, but I would venture to say he cherished that finish as much (if not more) than the Ethiopian -- Tsegaye Kebede – who set a new course record (2:04.38) about six hours earlier.

"Iron sharpens iron..." Terry sharpened me on that course too – and, once again, all I can think to say – to him, to the dedicated Team In Training local and national staff, to our fellow coaches and mentors – is: "I'm honored."

This book is a tribute to an organization that hundreds of thousands of people hold dear and credit, in numerous cases, with changing their lives. The athlete stories and interviews are all genuine; the creative writer in Dan McCann conjured the "airplane conversation" used throughout the book – an amalgam of the dozens of airplane conversations he's had since his Team In Training journey began. And, what a journey it has been. One step, followed by another...

Two

The Information Meeting

"I had a few co-workers who'd joined this crazy group called Team In Training. So, when I received that purple flyer in the mail, I thought, 'I can do that. I can run 13.1 miles and raise some money.'

"Then, as I sat in the information meeting, I started to get worried. What was I getting myself into?! I had never run more than three miles. Could I actually do this? And there, I started one of the most amazing journeys of my life..." – **Samantha Cody, TNT athlete**

I can picture it vividly: The frosted grass crunching beneath my feet, my pace quickening as I draw closer, a single tear tracking down my face. A tear of joy – and sadness.

I will kneel down to speak with her, my right knee settling in the manicured grass, my finger tracing the path of the engraved marble: Sharon McCann Bearden – Sept. 3, 1966 - Feb. 6, 2005. 38 years old. Survived by her husband and two daughters.

"We did it, sis," I will say. "All of those athletes. All of those races. All of that money raised. We did it."

And with that, my composure will disappear – and I will contain the tears no more.

Someday.

"Business or pleasure?"

"What's that?" I said with a slight smile, jolted from my pre-flight meditation.

"Business or pleasure?" my row-mate repeated as he fumbled for his lap-belt and turned toward me in his seat. "Are you heading to San Diego for business or pleasure?"

Judging from his blazer, buttoned-down shirt, and the laptop case he'd crammed into the overheard, I quickly surmised he was coming or going on the clock.

"A bit of both," I nodded politely – and the introvert inside pondered leaving it at that. Plane chatter? Normally, not my thing.

"Good afternoon, ladies and gentleman," the captain crooned from the cockpit. "Welcome aboard American Airlines flight 22-14 with service from Dallas to San Diego. Flight time today? Just under three hours."

He paused for a second and continued: "Sunny and 85 in San Diego right now with winds out of the South, 7 miles-per-hour. Take-off here in just a few minutes. Once again, welcome aboard."

Just under three hours... I had already perused the in-flight magazine during "leg one" – Omaha to Dallas – and, over the past few minutes, sufficiently enjoyed the comfort of my thoughts and the view of the back of seat 19A. My time before take-off was free, and my mood was light – so I ventured into conversation.

"What about you?" I asked. "Are you heading home or heading out?"

"Heading out," he said. "I'm attending a bio-fuels conference in San Diego. I'm an engineer with Texas Biotech in Arlington."

He paused. I shook my head and did that little frowny-thing with my lips indicating I was not familiar.

"Our company takes used vegetable oil and turns it into biodiesel – fuel of the future," he said.

"No kidding," I replied with a sniff.

"What about you?" he asked. "What's your business?"

"I'm a freelance writer," I answered, "and my wife and I coach marathoners for a group called Team In Training. We have athletes running in the Rock 'n' Roll Marathon on Sunday, and I was up in the travel rotation."

"Team In Training?" he inflected. Now he was unsure.

I'm not the best judge, but my fellow traveler appeared to be early-to-mid 50's – about 10 years older than me – with a round, unintimidating face, meaty hands and a bit of a paunch in the mid-section. Some might immediately assume he was not a runner. Not me. I am well aware that runners come in all shapes and sizes – and the ones you think might be "back of the pack" can wind up blowing you away.

"Yeah, it's a pretty amazing deal," I began. "Team In Training is the world's largest charity endurance sports training program and a real fundraising powerhouse for the Leukemia & Lymphoma Society."

The Genesis of the Leukemia & Lymphoma Society

"*The Leukemia & Lymphoma Society (LLS) was born out of a family's grief following the death of their teenage son.*

"*Robert Roesler de Villiers, son of a well-to-do New York family, was only 16 when he quickly succumbed to leukemia in 1944. Five years later, frustrated by the lack of effective treatments for what was then considered a hopeless disease, parents Rudolph and Antoinette de Villiers started a fundraising and education organization in their son's name.*

"*Headquartered in a small Wall Street office, the Robert Roesler de Villiers Foundation had only a few volunteers and a tiny budget. The task was daunting. Most leukemia patients, especially children, died within three months. ... Driven by the de Villiers' nearly boundless belief that leukemia and other blood cancers were indeed curable, the Foundation grew steadily, opening its first chapters in the New York City area. The organization, after changing its name to The Leukemia Society, was renamed The Leukemia Society of America in the 1960s to communicate a broad, national reach.*"[3]

---

[3] www.lls.org

The flight attendants made one last pass through the cabin checking for reclined seats, downed tray tables and electronics holdouts. I felt the plane jolt as it started to pull from the gate.

"The Leukemia & Lymphoma Society," my row-mate responded, "I know the organization, but I've never heard of Team In Training."

"The idea is pretty simple," I explained. "Your friends, your neighbors, your co-workers – people just like you and me – sign on for an event: a half or full marathon, a triathlon, a cycle ride or a hike. They basically agree to up-end their lives for 4-to-5 months, squeezing in their training between family, work, school and all the rest – before sunrise, after sunset, heat of summer, cold of winter... They endure the blisters, the chafing, the black toenails – and the comfort-zone-crushing-task of asking family, friends and co-workers for money to support LLS and its mission..."

"You're really selling it," he interjected.

"Here's the upside," I continued. "In return for their commitment, they're going to receive coaching from a certified someone like me, support from dedicated staff, fundraising guidance from alumni mentors, an expenses-paid event weekend, and an experience that, if they are open to it, will transform their lives dramatically. Forever."

"Where do I sign up?" he said with a chuckle.

"It all starts," I replied, "at the information meeting."

The information meeting. The proverbial first step in this journey of hundreds of thousands of miles and more than $1.4 billion raised – money that supports lifesaving research, patient services (including patient financial aid and co-pay assistance programs), community services, education and advocacy.

Any staffer, any coach, any mentor who's been with TNT for a while has spent their fair share of time at information meetings, mingling with potential recruits in conference rooms and coffee shops, educating them about this remarkable organization – where their fundraising dollars go – and whether it's really worth it to devote the next 16-20 weeks of their life to this endeavor. Videos, featuring enthusiastic alums and staff, tout Team In Training as "a way of life," and "more than just a Team; it's a family."

Oftentimes, the parents of a TNT "honored hero" or the "honored hero" themselves – typically a child who has experienced the ravages of cancer first-hand – will drive home the importance of the mission by detailing how the Leukemia & Lymphoma Society has assisted them in their journey toward recovery, remission or cancer freedom.

"Some attendees look on and nod politely, ask their questions, and leave without signing up," I told my fellow traveler. "Others fill out their paperwork, take a deep breath – and that leap of faith – and brace themselves. Most have no endurance event experience. 'That's okay,' we re-assure, 'we specialize in the fabulous first-timer.'"

Athlete Reflections:
"How Can I Not?"
– Jen Kwasny, TNT athlete

For Jen, the Team in Training experience has never been about one event or one moment, but one cause – a cure for blood cancers.

Her first event, the 2006 Nike Women's Half Marathon, was in memory of a good friend who passed away in 2005 from chronic myelogenous leukemia (CML), a cancer of the bone marrow and blood.

"For me, the Team experience starts at the information meeting; that is my 'singular' moment every time," she said. "I hear someone's story, how current drugs are working, how they were cured, or how they are still battling and refusing to give up. That's when I have my 'how can I not' moment.

"Every event I do with Team In Training is all about 'How can I not?'
- How can I not sacrifice a few days a week to train?
- How can I not give time to raise funds for a cure?

- How can I not run up that last hill when someone is receiving chemotherapy?
- How can I not donate to a cause that does such great work?

"It will always be that way. Through Team In Training, I have been fortunate to meet many people – and touch many lives – that I otherwise wouldn't have. I have friends who've joined Team; I've started an annual charitable hockey event; and I have a 17-year-old son who now wants to do charity events because, he says, 'How can I not?'

"Team In Training and all that happens when you join, can't be summed up for me in one singular moment in time. I haven't signed up for my next event yet, but I will soon – because how can I not?"

The information meeting is the first date in what promises to be a long, fulfilling relationship. We are strangers now, but that'll change over the course of the next 4-to-5 months. Our relationship will evolve. We will laugh, cry, struggle and achieve – together.

The Team In Training Model

"Once you sign up with Team In Training, you'll be training with our huge network of certified coaches who will have weekly group runs with you and your team. You'll even have mentors for fundraising support as well as your own website for online fundraising.

"In exchange for training and support, you help raise money towards cures for blood cancers like leukemia – the No. 1 disease killer of children – lymphoma and myeloma.

"As the largest endurance sports training program in the world, we will provide you with the experience of a lifetime."[4]

---

[4] www.teamintraining.org

Athlete's Journey:
Shambra L. Clifford's Story – Part I

To this day, Shambra still has that Team In Training flyer.

She received it in the mail during her freshman year of college, two things capturing her attention right away: the word "Run" in bold, blue lettering (she was a cross country runner in high school and had just joined the college team) and The Leukemia & Lymphoma Society logo (her brother was a survivor after spending eight years of his childhood battling leukemia).

Though she was not able to join at the time, she read up on the organization, became fascinated and stored that flyer away.

Five years later, while living in San Diego, CA, a desire to rev back up after a running break transferred the memory of that flyer – and that organization – from the back of her mind to the front. She went to an information meeting, a bit intimidated, not knowing what to expect.

"Walking in, I was surrounded by so many different people who were really passionate about this organization. After listening to the presenter and watching the video, I was instantly touched by the stories of survivors and loved ones left behind. Their mission was to make things just a bit easier for those going through situations all too familiar.

"I joined the Team that night – not quite sure if I could accomplish the program and my first half marathon, assured (genuinely it seemed) that I could."

―――

Athlete's Journey:
Julie Petersen's Story – Part I

Julie attended her first Team In Training information meeting in January 2005, about five months after her 29-year-old husband felt a lump in one of his testicles. **Cancer.**

"I was terrified – for my husband, for our family – but I could not let him see it. I had to be strong," Julie said. "I had to find a way to show him that I supported him wholeheartedly; that I was going through this **with** him, not just beside him. But, how? What could I possibly do to show him that I would endure anything so that he felt like he was not alone?"

Team In Training.

But, could she do it? Could she push her body to the limits and complete a triathlon without giving up?

Julie was determined to find out...

**Coaches' Inbox:
Taking the Leap**

Coaches,

I am super excited, a bit nervous, and pretty impressed with myself for signing up!

I started running (slogging is more accurate) in May of 2011. I followed the Omaha Running Club's "Step into Running" program. I have NEVER been an athlete. Not even barely. But, I lost 80 lbs. in the last year (still have more to go) and finally got the confidence to TRY running. I was encouraged (forced) by a friend to do the program over the summer and have LOVED it ever since.

What I gained from that experience was a whole lot of confidence in myself, and I let go of a lot of insecurities I had. I really don't care if I am the last one done, crawling across the finish line. I'm out there, and I did more than the millions sitting home on the couch. I've become a good example for my two girls, and they are proud of me. It also helped me see my own body as the strong, capable, amazing machine that is worthy of being treated well!

With the end of the 5K race season, I really thought that taking a casual approach to my fitness was what I wanted until next spring. In the last few months, I've realized that isn't really a good thing for me. A goal, a team, a coach, SOMETHING is needed for me to keep working.

Then the TNT flyer came in the mail...

My sister was diagnosed with thyroid cancer 2 1/2 years ago. She is healthy, doing well, and still LIVING with the disease. It is such a helpless feeling to have a loved one go through something like this. I wanted to beat the hell out of cancer – a bully tormenting my little sister – but couldn't.

Even though TNT is not, specifically, for thyroid cancer, I feel like I am doing SOMETHING – to honor those who've died, who are living, and to also honor God for giving me this body.

Plus, I REALLY want one of those "13.1" stickers for the car!

Again, thank you so much for your time & support! I can't wait to really get going on this.

Drawing ever closer to take-off, I confided in my row-mate: "It really is amazing the number of stories we've heard – too many to count – of fate connecting athlete to Team In Training at just the right time: *and then the Team In Training Flyer came in the mail...*

"One of the Nebraska Chapter's great former coaches, a woman named Shari, told the now legendary story of an athlete who, before joining the Team, was at a low in his life – an overweight smoker with no confidence and no direction. At his breaking point, out to dinner with friends, a waitress walked by, and in her wake, a TNT flyer floated to the table. He asked the waitress if it was hers. It wasn't. Where it came from he didn't know, but it came and he allowed it to be the call to action he needed to ignite change in his life, change for the greater good. Today, that person is a marathoner."

I continued, "Sometimes, we find Team In Training for ourselves. Sometimes, it finds us."

Athlete Journey:
Katie Sullivan Poppert's Story – Part I

While perusing her inbox one night, Katie came across the email that would shape the rest of her summer.

And change her life.

It was an ad inviting women to a Team In Training information meeting, encouraging them to participate in the Nike Women's Marathon in San Francisco while raising money for the Leukemia & Lymphoma Society. The email arrived just weeks after Katie's best friend, Christy, a lymphoma survivor, had officially finished her treatments.

"It got my attention because they mentioned that there would be free massages, chocolate, wine, and firemen at the meeting. I mean, really? Is there any better way to target women?" Katie, an oncology nurse, recalled.

At the time, Christy was in Florida with her family, relaxing on the beach and enjoying the lack of medical appointments. Katie called her – and then signed them both up to attend.

"The meeting took place in this funky old Denver Victorian, and we immediately helped ourselves to some wine and chocolate and got in line for our massages. There were probably fifty ladies there, and everyone had a story to tell about why they were interested in Team In Training. The biggest surprise to me was the number of women who were not actually affected by cancer, but wanted to help and needed the training.

"As we made our way upstairs to the conference room, I was looking around at the fit group of people gathered there, and I had my first doubts as to whether I could pull this off. I mean, what was I thinking? Here I was, with a fused SI joint in my pelvis, actually contemplating completing a marathon. Must have been all the wine and chocolate," Katie said.

Still, she and Christy filled out all the paperwork. Christy would run her race; Katie would walk.

As they headed home, excited and unsure about what they'd just signed up for, the task ahead began to sink in.

"We had to raise $4200 each in order to compete in the half marathon," Katie explained. "How in the heck were we going to be able to raise that kind of money? And how in the heck did I think I was going to be able to walk my way across that finish line, when merely walking to the park with the kids would have my feet up for the rest of the afternoon?"

Blood Cancer By the Numbers

- *Approximately every 4 minutes one person in the United States is diagnosed with a blood cancer.*
- *An estimated combined total of 149,990 people in the US are expected to be diagnosed with leukemia, lymphoma or myeloma in 2013.*
- *New cases of leukemia, lymphoma and myeloma are expected to account for 9.0 percent of the estimated 1,660,290 new cancer cases diagnosed in the US in 2013.*
- *An estimated 1,129,813 people in the US are living with, or are in remission from, leukemia, lymphoma or myeloma.*[5]

Team In Training Spotlight: The Genesis of TNT – The Cleland Story

Trace the genealogy of Team In Training and the path will lead to a father named Bruce Cleland; his daughter Georgia, a leukemia survivor; and a rag-tag team of 38 people cobbled together to train for the 1988 New York City Marathon – and raise potentially life-saving funds for the Leukemia Society of America (LSA), precursor to the Leukemia & Lymphoma Society. That inaugural group raised an astounding $322,000 for LSA's

---

[5] www.lls.org

Westchester/Hudson Valley Chapter – and, like that, Team In Training was born.

The week before Easter 1986. Georgia Cleland, two years and three months old, had been unwell, off and on, for a couple of weeks. Normally bright and cheery, she was pale now and crying a lot. Young children often cut teeth at that age and catch a lot of bugs, father Bruce reasoned.

Still, Georgia's mother, Izzi, insisted on taking her to the pediatrician day after day. Nothing was diagnosed. Several times over that period, coming home late from work in New York, Bruce would tell his English wife that she should let Georgia be, that she (Izzi) was fussing too much, that there was nothing wrong. But Izzi persisted.

The Thursday before Easter – hours before Izzi and the kids were booked on a flight to see Izzi's family in London – the concerned mother insisted on taking Georgia back to the doctor. One last visit. Again, Bruce urged her not to worry, to just get on the plane and enjoy the Easter break.

"Izzi's persistence probably saved Georgia's life," Bruce said.

Bruce was working in his office when he received Izzi's tearful call – a tumble of information he would never forget: blood work – an off-the-chart white blood cell count – a daughter diagnosed with acute lymphoblastic leukemia (ALL), the most common type of cancer in children from 1 to 7 years old.

"At that time, in my mind, the word 'leukemia' simply meant 'death,'" Bruce said.

An icy chill went down his spine as he reached for his coat and ran from the office –speaking to no one. From there on, it was a blur of fear, apprehension, paralyzing frustration.

"We were so used to managing our lives and circumstances independently, but now we were facing an impossibly frightening situation over which we had no control. I still remember, so clearly, the pediatrician saying, 'I don't mean to frighten you, but you must understand that your lives will never be the same again.' I don't think we really understood what he meant at that time, but it's been so true," Bruce recalled. "Georgia's leukemia changed our lives profoundly, and it will continue to affect us for the rest of our lives."

An Idea Starts to Form

The weeks after Georgia Cleland's diagnosis were frantic with worry. But after several very scary days and aggressive chemotherapy, her cancer went into remission and, from then on, the Clelands were involved in the maintenance phase of their daughter's disease.

Izzi was Georgia's primary care-giver. Bruce had just started a new business and was working hard to make it succeed – but he needed more. He needed something to balance his work and better connect with Georgia's illness. So, in June 1986, he and Izzi contacted the Westchester chapter of what was then the Leukemia Society of America (LSA) and offered to get involved in their research fundraising efforts.

They took to it immediately. So many friends had asked how they could help, and here was a way. At first, the Cleland's assisted with events organized by others, but they soon began organizing their own events, including a black tie ball that included the raffle of a donated car.

"These events were quite successful, a lot of hard work but very therapeutic. The problem was – we had to keep going back to the same group of friends to ask for their financial support. One day, a very good friend told me, 'It sure is expensive to be your friend.' He was right," Bruce said.

He continued, "These events also required so much hands-on human capital that they were not really scalable, so I found myself musing on ways we could use leverage, the same way we do in business, to reach a wider community of participants and donors."

The wheels were starting to turn.

Sitting around at 3 o'clock in the morning after a successful black tie ball in 1987, absolutely exhausted and reflecting on the event, Bruce looked down at his somewhat substantial stomach, and he was struck, then and there, by the awful shape he was in. The native New Zealander had always been fairly athletic, but surgery on his left knee (fallout from an old rugby injury) had prevented him from running the last few years. That and working too hard meant he had let himself go for too long.

His thoughts drifted to the recently run New York City Marathon and to a New Zealand friend named Rod Dixon, a world-class runner, Olympic medalist and NYC Marathon winner (1983). Rod, his wife and their two daughters had stayed with the Clelands from time to time at their home in Rye, NY. "I'd love to be able to run a marathon, but there's no way with these buggered knees," Bruce remembered thinking.

Enter Bob Wieland, a Vietnam veteran who had lost both legs, all the way up to his torso, to a landmine. The New York Post ran a profile about Wieland and how he competed in endurance events – not in a wheelchair but on a small skateboard-like structure that he propelled using his arms and two hand-worn wooden rockers. In 1986, it took him four days, two hours, 48 minutes, and sixteen seconds to finish the NYC Marathon. He completed the 1987 race in three days, nine hours, thirty seven minutes, and forty five seconds – an improvement of more than one day!

Bruce couldn't stop thinking about that article, about Bob Wieland. Here Bruce was with four mainly good limbs and just a couple of bad knees – surely there was some way he could run a marathon.

The Birth of TNT

"You've got to be f*****g crazy!"

That was the initial response Bruce received upon calling a Kiwi buddy in Los Angeles, Geoff Andrews, a former rugby player with bad knees – and a very big heart. Bruce had spent a sleepless night thinking about marathoning and Wieland – and that's when the basic idea for TNT poured out in a jumble of thoughts:

- Could he find a group of "former athletes," like him, who were out of shape but wished they weren't? People who would love the opportunity to become members of a "team" and physically transform themselves into marathon runners?

- Could they create some real human interest in that idea?

- Could they get corporate and individual sponsors to support them on a scale that would enable them to raise some really serious money for Leukemia research?

- Could he get his friend Rod Dixon involved as their team coach?

After spilling out that jumble of thoughts to Geoff – and abruptly getting hung up on – Bruce realized that 7 a.m. in New York was 4 a.m. in LA. A few hours later, a less groggy Geoff called back and asked Bruce to repeat the idea.

"When I finished explaining it, he said 'I think you're absolutely bloody crazy, but if you do it, I'll do it,' and at that moment, I knew that as long as there were two of us, we had a 'team,'" Bruce said.

His next call was to Rod Dixon who was back living in New Zealand.

"Rod listened to his idea, and said that while he wouldn't always be able to be there to train the team, he would love to be part of it," Bruce recalled.

Rod suggested that he might be able to get some of his other running mates involved, including Eamon Coughlin, the Irish runner and world indoor mile record-holder who happened to live in Rye, the same town as the Clelands.

At that point, Bruce sensed they had something viable – it was just a question of getting others interested. 40 runners, he guessed, would be as many as he could manage and coordinate, so he made several phone calls and encouraged friends to call friends. Pretty soon, they had their 40, which included two friends from Switzerland and three from England.

"Early on, it occurred to me that many of the 40 were quite badly out of shape, and that we had better be careful. I called my attorney and asked him to prepare a liability disclaimer. The next call went to our family pediatrician and a close family friend, Norm Berkowitz, the doctor who had diagnosed Georgia. I told Norm about the idea, and asked if he would like to run with us. He said he wouldn't be able to run, but he would be happy to serve as our team physician," Bruce said.

The time came to start training. A Sunday afternoon in February 1987 – all of the recruits gathered in a church hall in Rye, where Bruce enlisted the help of Suzie Joyce, an aerobics instructor friend, to take them through their first workout.

It was not a pretty sight.

Part way through the session, Suzie and Dr. Berkowitz called Bruce aside: "We need to talk." They were concerned that several members of the team were in very poor physical shape, and there was no way that they could safely run a marathon.

They abandoned the workout for that day in favor of some gentle stretching while Norman gave each participant a quick, five minute check-up. He told many of them to make appointments with their personal physicians to get a proper medical clearance. Some never returned.

From that point on, it all began to fall into place, but Bruce and company were flying completely blind.

"We had no blueprint and were making it up as we went along. So, we did what endurance athletes do – we just kept putting one foot in front of the other and let it take shape," he said.

A friend in the advertising business came to Bruce's home one rainy Sunday afternoon to discuss the program and decided on a name for the endeavor. "Team In Training" it was. They sketched out a rough logo and designed a small brochure to be used as a mailing piece, explaining what they were doing and listing the names of all the members of the team. It also included photographs of Rod Dixon, Leonard Marshall (NY Giants), and Gary Carter (NY Mets) who had all agreed to lend their names to the event.

All the while, Bruce and his business partner were building a new business they had launched in May 1986. They had a small office in the World Trade Center, really just a place for their 35 traders and brokers to meet before the markets opened and in the afternoon after the markets closed. The rest of the day, they were all working on the floor of the commodities exchanges in New York.

Their office quickly became "mission control" for the fledgling TNT program, and at times, it felt like Grand Central Station. Calls came in from all over the country and all over the world. They were swamped with people asking how they could help and where they could send their checks.

"As the momentum began to build, it was amazing to see the powerful effect of the 'law of large numbers.' 40 team members each spoke with 50 friends or business associates, and some of those people spoke to others, and then they all started mailing in checks. We became so overwhelmed that, eventually, we had to redirect all the correspondence to the Leukemia Society's Westchester Chapter office. Rochelle Kaufman, the executive director there, hired an assistant to deal with it all," Bruce said.

Along the way, they decided to hold a pre-race "pump-up party" the night before the race and a post-race "victory reception" after the race. They recruited friends as volunteers to organize those events.

Finally, the day of the race arrived.

After all of the training and all the tears – and with a great deal of difficulty for many of them – every TNT team member who started the race finished. The victory reception was held at the San Moritz Hotel on Central Park South in New York, and it was at that reception that it really dawned on them just how much money they had raised – over $320,000. They also calculated that collectively they had lost more than half a ton of weight!

"When I look back on it now, I can't quite believe how we did it. Logistically it was so difficult because we had no support or infrastructure and no email, internet or cell phones with which to stay in close contact with all those people for 10 months," Bruce recalled.

A few weeks after the race, Dwayne Howell, then-President of LSA, called to congratulate Bruce on their success and asked him to meet with him and his colleagues in New York to explain how they had done it. After that meeting, Dwayne and his colleagues used that information to compile a "how to" handbook that explained the whole process.

Subsequently, a decision was made to make TNT the LSA's "signature event" and roll it out nationally. The LSA put together a dedicated staff in New York to coordinate TNT nationally and the handbook was distributed to LSA Chapters around the country...

– **Contributed by Bruce Cleland, TNT founder**. *(Cleland was honored by Runner's World magazine in 2004 as one of their "Heroes of Running" for his role in establishing TNT.)*

The Battle against Cancer:
On the Front Lines

Meet cancer fighter Wendy Sontag, MSW, LISW, Patient Services Manager, Leukemia & Lymphoma Society-Iowa Chapter

Of the money raised by Team In Training athletes and other Leukemia & Lymphoma Society fundraising streams (Light the Night, Man & Woman of the Year, Pennies for Patients), 25 percent is spent on research ventures. 50 percent supports patient and community services, a menu that includes:
- Financial aid programs
- Emotional support connections
- Public education
- Professional education
- Information referral or educational information

Tell us about some of the patient and community services programs that LLS provides through Team In Training funds.

What prompts the most calls to us is patient financial assistance, which is divided into two parts. The first part is **general patient aid**. With this program, patients receive a one-time $100 stipend to offset costs. All that is required to apply for the program is a doctor's signature or certification that they do have a blood cancer. They do not have to provide claims or provide any other documentation. It is based on the honor system. It's important for Team In Training participants to know that some of their fundraising goes directly into the pockets of people who need it the most. It is a direct gift. We are still the only voluntary health organization non-profit that provides a grant available to any patient who applies.

The second part of the program is the **Co-Pay Assistance Program.** Reimbursement amounts vary based on diagnosis. A lymphoma diagnosis, for example, carries of potential reimbursement of up to $2,500; and of up to $10,000 for myeloma.

The application process for this program is more involved, there are some income eligibility requirements. Once approved for the program, patients have to provide supporting documentation for their claims: reimbursement for medication claims, co-pays for insurance premiums coverage or co-pays for doctor visits when they have received chemotherapy.

The program is administered by a third party on a national basis. LLS solicited sponsors for the program to reserve more money for research.

We had close to 90 patients in Nebraska that availed themselves of that program in 2012, and it amounted to over $200,000 that was received in just Nebraska. It's made a huge difference for a lot of people with their prescription coverage and some of those high co-pays for the oral chemotherapy drugs that are so outrageously expensive.

What is the First Connection Program?
This is my favorite part of patient services. It is a huge source of hope for people and one of the Leukemia & Lymphoma Society's most popular and effective support programs. It is a free LLS service that connects patients and their loved ones with a trained peer volunteer who has gone through a similar experience. Often referred to as 'First Connection,' the program is named after Patti Robinson Kaufmann, a Colorado lymphoma patient who lost her battle in 2008.

Do you have an example of how the First Connection Program has helped a patient that you can share?
We had a patient who did not want to continue with treatment. So, we asked a volunteer who had thought of not completing treatment – but did – to make contact with that patient. I think we could say that volunteer saved that patient's life by giving them that call and by nature of who they are. It is not the doctor or nurse telling them that they need to do treatment; it's another patient. It gives them that little bit of motivation that they need to go on with their treatment plan even at the lowest time. I think that is really a powerful thing.

I may have a young mom who is going through treatment and wants to talk with someone else who had young children when she went through chemotherapy. So then, it is not so much about the diagnosis as it is the social situation – how do you care for your young children when you're having chemotherapy? We will set them up with another volunteer who had young children when they were diagnosed.

There is a volunteer in south central Nebraska who's lived with myeloma for over ten years. Not too long ago, a prognosis for myeloma was not more than five years. So, the fact that he is alive and patients can talk to him is, again, a great source of hope.

In addition to First Connections, LLS also facilitates face-to-face support groups and telephone support groups, which meet the needs of people who may be more isolated or don't have access to a face-to-face group. For older folks who maybe don't want to go out at night or who aren't feeling well enough to go out, they can be part of the group from the comfort of their home. It's free, and it's easy.

All of our groups are facilitated by qualified oncology professionals that have been vetted by LLS. We try to ideally have a social worker and a nurse facilitator so we cover both the emotional support and the educational piece for the members.

How does LLS help people with blood cancers get to information and education about their illnesses?
One of the things I always stress to people is we do have the free 800 number for our information resource center: **1-800-955-4572**. The people who answer the line are Masters level oncology professionals. They have a medical library right at their fingertips. Sometimes I refer healthcare professionals to them, and certainly patients can call and get specific about their diseases and treatment options.

We also offer a lot of information on our website (www.lls.org) and in our treatment booklets and disease-specific booklets. Some of those are updated every 12-18 months, depending upon if treatments are changing. We get a lot of feedback that they are helpful and user friendly. All of the booklets can be downloaded from the LLS website. Treatment sites can also order books from local chapter or national chapter in large quantities.

Three

Why We Team

"Team sports were never my strong suit, hence the initial appeal of running when I first went to college. The success (or failure) of a workout was dependent on just one person, the girl I saw in the mirror. Something about this independent sport was enough to hold me accountable to becoming a healthier, stronger, and more confident person.

"After five years of building my skills as a runner, my long term goal of running a full marathon was becoming more and more appealing – but I was also unable to find the necessary motivation to begin training and actually sign up for a race.

"It was around this time that I first heard of Team In Training. From that point forward, being part of a team would never be or mean the same to me..." – **Mackenzie Raber, TNT athlete**

Now at the front of the line for take-off, our plane started gradually, steadily picking up speed as it prepared to break the bounds of gravity. The Dallas landscape began to blur. I brought some work with me, but it could wait. I was in a mood to talk TNT – and my fellow traveler still seemed willing to engage.

"Have you always been a runner?" he inquired as we lifted from terra firma.

"Hardly," I laughed. "After college until about age 30, I was basically on 'exercise hiatus.' Nine years of eating, sleeping, sitting at a desk and watching a lot of TV. I remember, pretty vividly, reaching that breaking point: Christmas time 2003 – I was eating cheesecake for breakfast and lunch, and it occurred to me, this was not how I envisioned my life playing out, some dude whose exercise regimen consisted of walking back and forth from the fridge for ice cream. Besides, I had two young sons at the time. I knew I needed to get healthy to keep up with them."

"And, what was your secret?" he asked.

"No secret really. No magic bullet," I said. "I finally read that copy of 'Body for Life' that had been gathering dust in my closet for years. I trimmed my portion sizes, cut out the junk six days a week, hit the gym and made peace with the treadmill. Just 20 minutes at first – and that was a brutal 20 minutes. But, it got easier and I got stronger. 12 weeks later, I was down about 35 pounds."

"Fantastic," he said.

I paused for a moment and looked out the window. That amazing expanse of the sky. The face of God. My thoughts trailed back to February 2005, flying home after the funeral, feeling so grateful to be that much closer to Heaven.

"In hindsight, I realized it was a complete 'God-thing,' His divine hand guiding me, preparing me for the trials ahead – the fallout of my sister's melanoma diagnosis – and what would be our prime coping mechanism. If I hadn't gotten myself together, I don't think I would have even considered Team In Training."

"And you joined the Team when?" he asked.

"As an athlete in late 2004. My wife, Kelly, actually paved the way, signing up in 2003. Her friend, Tricia, was in the running circles and had gone to one of those information meetings. She told Kelly about it, said all she needed to bring were some Kleenex and her registration fee – and she was right."

Athlete Reflections:
"Little Did I Know How Much It Would Help Me too"
– Kelly McCann, TNT run coach/athlete

"After seeing the videos and hearing about the hope and the fight that was going on, how could I not join?" Kelly recalled.

At that point, she had little confidence in herself as a runner – not much of a history to draw from other than two half marathons. But, she figured, if given the opportunity for support and guidance, she would take full advantage and sign up for a full marathon – San Diego Rock 'n' Roll 2004.

"I had to face the unknown to push my limits just as Sharon was facing the unknown in her own battle. When she was diagnosed with melanoma, I felt pretty helpless and out-of-control. I wanted to show her that I believed in her, in her efforts to fight this. If we were in this battle together, we could give each other strength, faith, and hope when the other one was being knocked around.

"It wasn't the exact same – no one but those who actually face the knife, the drugs, the radiation, the lasers, the fatigue, and the fear first hand can truly compare war stories. But it was all I had to offer. I started out doing it for her – little did I know how much it would help me too..."

Athlete Reflections:
"Who Can Say No to Their Big Sister?"
– Mike McAtee, TNT athlete

Mike's call to "the great purple cause" came over the radio one cold January morning. He was on his way into work, firmly in "hope mode."

His sister, Karren, was battling **chronic lymphoid leukemia** (**CLL**), the most common type of **leukemia**. Regular chemo treatments that kept her disease in check were now failing, and her doctor was now recommending a bone marrow transplant.

You'd think with four siblings at her disposal, one would be a match.

Nope. None of them. (Unfortunately at the time, two of Mike's brothers were unable to donate because they were engaged in cancer battles of their own; one of them also fighting leukemia.)

So, into "hope mode" he went:

- Hoping that Karren's current chemo would keep her alive long enough for another, more effective treatment to be found;

- Hoping she would find a match from the bone marrow donor registry (which Mike signed up for right away).

It was beginning to seem like "hoping" was all he could do – until he heard about TNT on the radio that January morning. Here was a program that would allow him to raise money for cancer research while doing something that was, also, good for his health.

"I do not want to diminish, in any way, my primary reason for joining the TNT family that year, but in hindsight, I recognize now that a big motivation for me was the physical challenge of participating in an endurance event," Mike said.

Even with all of that motivation, he still had doubts about signing up. But, it wasn't the prospect of training that concerned him (though he was admittedly out-of-shape and overweight).

It was the prospect of asking other people for money. While he had given to many charities over the years, he, personally, never raised a dime for charity in his life.

"I count myself as a quiet, introspective, self-reliant guy, and I knew that asking people for money, even for a great cause, would be a challenge," Mike recalled. "I actually remember thinking, 'If the fundraising doesn't work out, I could always dig deep into the family finances and come up with the money.'" (Turns out, Mike easily met his goal through a letter writing campaign, and in the process discovered how willing and generous people are – one only need ask.)

He now looks back on his decision to join TNT – and train for the Hy-Vee Triathlon in Des Moines – as the start of a new chapter in his life.

"I experienced a feeling of camaraderie and sense of purpose that I hadn't experienced since my days in the military," he said.

He continued, "My event weekend was fantastic. I flew my sister out from California, had my wife, my children, my grandchildren and some of my closest friends at the event. The race venue was unlike any other I had ever seen, complete with grandstands on either side of the finishing chutes that led to the grand finishing line arch."

As he sprinted (after more than 3 hours of swimming, biking and running) across that line, his sister and the rest of his family were in the stands cheering him on.

"Okay, so role credits and cue the music, story over right? Nope it gets better," he said.

Two months after his event, Mike received an email from the Leukemia & Lymphoma Society which profiled a CLL patient who participated in the clinical trial of a revolutionary drug called Rituxan®, developed with the help of LLS funding.

Rituxan®: A Targeted Therapy for Lymphoma Patients

Rituxan®, a monoclonal antibody drug, was FDA approved for follicular non-Hodgkin lymphoma (NHL) patients in 1997. In fact, it was the very first targeted drug approved in the U.S. LLS-funded researchers found that Rituxan® can dramatically improve chemotherapy effectiveness, and the FDA approved Rituxan® to be used in combination with other chemotherapy drugs for people with follicular lymphoma and other non-Hodgkin lymphoma types. It's contributed to a doubling of the survival rate for NHL patients, and is now also FDA approved as a treatment for patients with chronic lymphocytic leukemia or Hodgkin lymphoma.[6]

"*The most important thing that has happened in lymphoma has probably been rituximab (U.S. brand name: Rituxan) for b-cell lymphomas. It has changed the world; it is an amazing thing.*" – **Dr. James (Jim) Armitage, an internationally recognized authority on non-Hodgkin**

---

[6] www.lls.org

lymphoma and the Joe Shapiro Professor of Medicine, University of Nebraska Medical Center

---

Mike immediately forwarded the email to his sister, asking her to check it out and, if her current treatment didn't included this drug, to ask her doctor about it.

Here's an excerpt from her reply, which Mike pulls out every year when he has his doubts about whether he can do another TNT event:

"Yes, I got this email as well, and YES, I was given Rituxan, Cytoxin and Fludarabin. The combo of all those drugs is what kicked that cancer's butt! In fact, a few months ago, my doctor called me to see if I would talk to one of her patients that has the same cancer as me to tell her about the treatments first hand, explain what she would go through, etc. She was Russian and had to have her daughter interpret for her. We had a three-way conference call going on, and it really made me feel good to calm her about her fears and that, yes, there would be side effects from the treatments, but I would go through it again if it ever became necessary.

"So you just keep running as long as you can brother dear, cuz we are living proof that the money that is donated to these foundations are put to good use in finding cures and treatments."

Today, Mike's sister has been cancer free for over four years from a single round of this treatment.

"So, why do I Team?" Mike offered, "I Team for the challenge, for my health, for the friendship and joy of training, but mostly, I Team to repay a debt to those that came before me, that raised the money that led to the development of the drug that saved my sister's life and the lives of so many others.

"I Team because there are not effective treatments for all individuals and that people die every year from these diseases still. I Team because it's my turn to inspire people to give so funds are available to help families in need and to do the research that leads to the next cure. Finally, I Team because my big sister said so – and who can say no to their big sister?"

Coaches' Inbox:
Why I Team

Coach,

I chose to run this marathon in Alaska for a number of reasons:

1) I hope to get into shape and tone up my body.

2) I want to feel healthy and confident in myself again because that feeling has gone away over the last year.

3) I love challenging myself, especially with something new.

4) I hope to keep marathon running as a way to keep healthy for the rest of my life.

5) I want a final bonding experience with my father before I go off to college, and I feel amazing about accomplishing that in a place he has always dreamed of going, all while honoring and giving back to my grandpa.

Hey there,

Coach here – I just want to say I am extremely touched by your reasons for joining the team and taking on this challenge. I think they are all unbelievably worthy, but, as a father of an almost teenager, I have a special affinity for "number 5." (I can tell I'm going to like "teaming" with you already.)

Beyond the bonding, this experience will change your life in wonderful ways. You will find wells of strength and determination you never knew existed – and that confidence in yourself, that "can do spirit" is going to blossom again. How's this for a blessing for me – I get to witness that right along with you!

You will have moments of doubt; moments of what did I get myself in to. But, that's my job: To remind you why you're doing this – that you can succeed – that you will succeed!

Work hard. Stay focused on the starting line and revel in the fact that you're doing something good for yourself and for the world around you.

Go Team!

Athlete Reflections:
"Only If I Run It for Team In Training!"
– Tasha Hunt, TNT athlete

After receiving a Team In Training brochure in the mail in January of 2012, Tasha quickly decided this was something she wanted to do. If her 60-year-old mother could undergo a bone marrow transplant and months of aggressive chemo for acute myeloid leukemia (AML), Tasha could run a marathon in her honor.

"I also wanted to give back," she said. "So many people had made donations for my mom, and the Leukemia & Lymphoma Society had helped our family during the difficult time."

That May, when Tasha completed the 2012 National Guard Marathon in Lincoln, Neb., her mom was there, cheering her on mile after mile.

"Every time I passed her, it gave me motivation to run faster and harder. She was standing on the sidelines as a cancer survivor," Tasha said.

She continued, "This was the first race I had ever run that wasn't for me. This race was for my mom. This race was for all of those battling cancer. This race was to find a cure. Running with a mission completely changes everything. You find strength where you never thought you had it. I ran with so much heart and mission that I crossed the finish line with a Boston Marathon qualifying time. But even better than that, was crossing the finish line with my mom waiting at the end.

"If it weren't for organizations such as the Leukemia & Lymphoma Society, the research wouldn't be happening to find a cure. Everyone keeps asking if I am going to run the Boston Marathon, and my response is, 'Only if I run it for Team In Training!'"

Saving Lives One Mile at a Time

- *The 5-year survival rate of Leukemia has gone from 14 percent in 1960-1963 to 57 percent in 2001-2007.*
- *44,600 people were expected to be diagnosed with Leukemia in 2011.*
- *Had that same number been diagnosed in the earlier time period, only 5,352 would have survived more than five years after diagnosis.*

But in 2011, approximately 57 percent or 25,422 people will be expected to survive more than five years from their Leukemia diagnosis date.[7]

"Simply put," said LLS Board member Brian Gillette, "that is a difference of 20,070 more lives, and just in the case of Leukemia. Five year survival rates for non-Hodgkin lymphoma are at 70 percent; Hodgkin lymphoma five year survival rates are at 86 percent. Myeloma survival rates are up significantly as well."

Team In Training Spotlight: Running through Grief – The Lucy Duffy Story

One of the members of Bruce Cleland's inaugural Team In Training team was Lucy Duffy, a woman who has experienced cancer from all angles and whose passion for the mission has vaulted her securely into the life story of Team In Training.

Lucy's husband, Allen, died of acute mylogenous leukemia in 1986, a time when there was practically no hope for survival. Lucy, herself, was diagnosed with breast cancer in November of 2010. She had a mastectomy that December followed by radiation that spring. Lucy, in her 70's at the time, recovered in good order and, as quickly as possible, was on her beloved, shiny red bike determined to catch up with her New England Team and get in shape for America's Most Beautiful Bike Ride around Lake Tahoe.

---

[7] "Facts 2012" published by the Leukemia & Lymphoma Society

Over the years, Lucy has raised well over $300,000 for LLS. She wrote "Running through Grief" as a personal necessity after Allen's death.

Allen won't be here to drive me over the Verrazano Bridge to Staten Island to the start of the New York Marathon this year. My 66-year-old-body balks a bit now while I train, but I still yearn for the exhilaration of finishing at least one more marathon. In marathoning, to finish is to win. While running in the cooling rain this August morning, I thought of the Marathon in '86 when finishing was winning in a very special way.

Allen survived to share that marathon day with me. He made it through the first horrible onslaught of chemotherapy after the diagnosis of leukemia in July of '85 when he was 54 years old.

Running sustained me. I lived in Allen's sterile hospital room that first summer of intense treatment. Wearing all white and face masks, the nurses, doctors and I struggled to help Allen. With ice rubs as tortuous to Allen as the raging fever, we tried to cool his burning body. The poison injected through the port in his chest to kill the cancer cells also destroyed his immunity to infection.

"And I ran."

Daily I ran. I ran out through the hospital corridors into the streets of New Haven. I ran and I gained strength.

In September of '85, Allen came home from the hospital a skeleton of himself. And I ran. The school year began, and I taught and I ran. The tension, the anxiety of Allen's condition, and the prognosis were overwhelming. I left the house each day to pound the certainty of the earth, to absorb the changes of the seasons, to fill my lungs with the good air, to keep strong for my husband and my children and me, to exult in my ability to keep putting one foot in front of the other no matter what. Running kept me on course. I ran through that fall, that winter, that spring, that summer of '86 and the next fall – and Allen ran with me in my heart.

After a year and a half of hospitalization, chemotherapy, spontaneous bleeding, middle of the night emergency room visits, innumerable blood and platelet transfusions, bone marrow tests, and the daily anxiety of uncertain blood counts, Allen was in remission, having outlived his life sentence by a year.

Lucy against Leukemia

One day while I ran, a thought came to me. I would run the New York Marathon and raise money for the Leukemia Society of America. I wrote a letter telling of my mission to friends and relatives thinking I might raise a couple hundred dollars. Allen was a bit embarrassed at first, but when the notes and money began pouring in, he got into the spirit. The project mushroomed. Allen became the accountant, totaling up the pledges and enjoying the accompanying notes of love and encouragement. Often confined to home with low blood levels, Allen savored the daily mail. He read and counted – and I ran.

It was marathon day in '86. Allen wasn't feeling tip top, but he was well enough to go to New York with me. Allen drove me over the Verrazano Bridge, and he kissed me. I hopped out of the car to join the hordes of runners crowding onto Staten Island to prepare for the start. Allen looked pale, and he was anxious that I would be all right. It is a long way, 26.2 miles. I was confident and imbued with my mission.

I wore a shirt that read, "Lucy against Leukemia." While I ran through all the boroughs of New York, I surveyed the crowd and handed out little self-made solicitations for our cause. I ran. I flew. I floated. Nothing could stop me.

At the 16 mile mark, just over the Queensborough Bridge on First Avenue and 65th Street, my family was waiting, and I paused for hugs and kisses. Two of my four sons joined me in Central Park to run the last two miles. Allen watched the marathon on TV from a hotel room. We were both heroes that day. He was alive, and I finished the marathon and raised over 20,000 dollars to fight leukemia.

Allen died a month later.

A giant wave of loss kept catching up with me and enveloping me. I cried and I ran.

A Call from Bruce Cleland

One day, Bruce Cleland from Rye, New York called me. His two year old daughter, Georgia, had leukemia. He and his wife Isobel organized a team of runners in the New York Marathon to raise money to fight leukemia – and called it Team In Training. I joined his effort. We raised over $300,000 that year. Team In Training is now a nationwide effort with the hope of raising over $51 million this year.

This fall, I will run again, more slowly now, but keeping one foot in front of the other. This time, I will run in honor of Jacky, a courageous twelve-year-old leukemic girl. She had a bone marrow transplant. Progress has been made in the battle against leukemia. She will survive.

I will keep running and I will survive also. The joy of the run, the joy that is life, continues.

-- Contributed by Lucy DeVries Duffy, copyright 1999

The Battle against Cancer:
On the Front Lines

Meet cancer fighter Dr. James (Jim) Armitage, an internationally recognized authority on non-Hodgkin lymphoma, the Joe Shapiro Professor of Medicine, University of Nebraska Medical Center

"Dr. Armitage and his team at the University of Nebraska Medical Center saved my husband's life and kept our family whole. He embodies the compassion, intelligence and drive of those medical professionals and researchers fighting back and preempting the return of leukemias, lymphomas, myeloma and related blood cancers." - **Judy Mansisidor, TNT athlete/mentor/interviewer**

What advice do you offer patients and families when they first come in or are facing a relapse of lymphoma?
The first thing I try to tell everybody is – I know who works for whom. That's me for you, not the other way around. In the end, it's always what

the patient wants that gets done. It's possible that I would feel strongly about it, but in the end it's the patient's body.

Obviously, when a cancer comes back, it's a more serious situation, and it does come back in some diseases more often than others. Then you have to decide what is best – is it better to take a cautious approach or a really aggressive approach? That depends on the patient, their age and how they feel about taking risks.

What are the three most important developments that you've seen over your career that have led to better treatments and outcomes of lymphoma patients?
The most important thing that has happened in lymphoma has probably been rituximab (U.S. brand name: Rituxan) for b-cell lymphomas. It has changed the world; it is an amazing thing.

If you go back farther, I suppose you would say combination chemotherapy was a really important idea, the concept that you could take drugs, combine them and use them all at once to kill all the cancers cells, not just keep them under control for a while. It worked in diseases like childhood leukemia and non-Hodgkin lymphoma.

New insights into biology have probably transformed our approach the most. Now we understand much more than before what it is actually wrong with the cells, which genes are being activated when they ought not or turned off when they ought to work. That allows us to have better insights into what treatments might work.

In the 1970's, after a stint in private practice, Dr. Armitage started the bone marrow transplant program at the University of Iowa. There he really explored an interest in lymphomas. He was later recruited to come to Nebraska and serve as Vice Chairman of Medicine at the University of Nebraska Medical Center.
One of the things I wanted to do here was organize a lymphoma study group. It took a while, but I did it. The Nebraska Lymphoma Study Group has been going on now for over 30 years. We have pieces of the tumors of pretty much everybody diagnosed with lymphoma in the region, and we have a way to get the follow-up data on thousands of

patients involved, and it's led to hundreds of publications about the findings.

When I came here, I didn't intend to do transplants anymore. But, we needed to start a program, and I figured if we were going to do it, it's going to have to be something that I find interesting. So, I focused on doing autologous transplants, which are transplants using the patient's own cells to treat patients with lymphoma. We were one of the first places in the world to focus on that. It's become a standard of therapy, and it has made our reputation on this lymphoma team here.

For a lymphoma, if we can do an "auto," I would always favor doing that because it is so much safer. The chances of dying from an auto transplant are less than one in 20, provided there is no other complication in treatment. Allogeneic Transplants (when you receive someone else's immune system) offer another option, but are more dangerous. Simply put, those new cells can see you as the "wrong body," and the new immune system can then attack you. But there are circumstances where an "allo" is the right thing to do.

°**Do you have examples of how your research about lymphomas has benefitted other types of cancer research?**
Lymphomas have had a big impact in a lot of areas because they've been easier to study and more responsive. So, the principles of curative therapy with medicines really came from studying leukemia and lymphomas, both in understanding the biology of the disease and recognizing that a lymphoma isn't just one disease; it's really multiple different things. That has applied to lots of other diseases such as breast cancer.

Which genes are behaving badly? That's been a general question. It started probably in lymphomas as much as anywhere else with the solid tumors, and it has applied more and more to other cancers.

The concept of bone marrow transplants with solid tumors developed with lymphomas and has been used in other areas.

The concept that you can cure a cancer with a few treatments was worked out in lymphomas as much as anywhere else. We have to give people all sorts of treatments, but if the cancer sensitivity of the drugs only requires a certain number of treatments, you can stop and it's gone. That's something we learned with lymphomas.

What are the most rewarding parts of your life's works and research?
My job is intellectually exciting. The diseases are interesting. The amount of biology that we've learned about lymphoma is unbelievable from what we knew 30 years ago, and the disease has changed in an extraordinary way.

We effectively care for people that we wouldn't have been able to before. We cure large numbers of people; it's been really exciting.

But, by far, the most rewarding part of my job is the patients I get to know. People are way braver than you think they might be. It's really interesting and enlightening. It makes you a better person. We think better of our species, generally speaking, to know people and watch them deal with hard things. That's easily the most rewarding.

Four

First Miles

"We did two miles today as a family – and it was hard! This journey is going to be a challenge for sure, but we are going to make it. LLS provides us with a great support team and an even bigger reason to cross the finish line.

We thank everyone for their support on this journey – and please know that your contributions to the cause mean more than we can ever express." **– Scott J. McCoid, TNT athlete (from his training blog)**

I flipped my tray table down as the flight attendant progressed up the aisle with her loaded drink cart. I don't usually talk this much – so the prospect of a glass of water had added appeal.

"I remember joining my wife Kelly on that first event weekend," I told my row-mate. "Just supporting her, I felt like a hero by extension – and I knew I wanted some of that for myself."

"Would you like something?" the flight attendant interjected politely.

"Just a cup of water, please," I said.

"Ginger ale," my fellow traveler replied.

As she readied our drinks, I continued, "Team In Training is for real. I remember the moment clearly when that occurred to me – I mean really occurred to me."

I took my water from the flight attendant and allowed my companion to settle his ginger ale before pushing into one of my favorite TNT stories:

I was mid-stroke in the middle of the somewhat polluted – but I don't really want to think about that – Hudson River, just minutes into my first ever TNT event, the 2005 Ford New York City Triathlon, a one mile swim, 25 mile bike and 6.2 mile run.

The current was good that July morning. Strong. We could have just flopped on our backs and crushed our best pool time.

Stroke. Stroke. Breathe. Every time I popped up for air, I could actually hear my family cheering for me from the walkway aligning the river.

Dan... Gurgle, gurgle, gurgle... Go... Gurgle, gurgle, gurgle... Dan...

I was doing this – an outrageous feat for a buttoned-down, former coach potato – and I was being fully supported by those loved ones I could hear – and, I'm convinced, by the one I could hear no longer. My sister Sharon was there. Five months after succumbing to melanoma, she was watching over me, ensuring my safety, sending subtle signs.

My biggest fear heading into the swim – and, by extension, my biggest fear about the event in total – was really quite basic. In my head, I played out a dismal chain of events that would start with leaky goggles. The ensuing trickle of water would disrupt my contact lenses, leaving me blinded in the middle of the Hudson River, fumbling to the swim finish and then fumbling the .25 of a mile back to the transition area, and then fumbling to find my bike (and spare pair of glasses) in a crowd of thousands of similar looking bikes. It would be a nightmare.

Stroke. Stroke. Breathe.

"Hey man, your goggles aren't leaking. Your contacts are going to be fine," I thought to myself.

As soon as that realization took root, a calm washed over me, and it happened. That very moment. A plastic wristband that I was wearing – similar to what a hospital patient wears around their wrist – snapped off and flittered into the depths of the Hudson.

Skeptics might write it off as cheap manufacturing or dismiss it as operator error, but, to me, it was an unmistakable sign, a spiritual endorsement that this remarkable organization called "Team In Training" was, indeed, for real – and that I was fully supported in my endeavor.

In preparation for the race, I had scribbled a simple tribute on that wristband. Just one word. **Sharon**. *As the plastic broke from my wrist, the message I received from my late sister, my honored hero was clear – "You're good now... You've got this."*

I took a sip of my water. "TNT is for real."

"That's a fabulous story," my row-mate said. "And you and your wife became coaches when?"

"2007," I answered.

"And you could get someone like me to complete a half marathon – or a marathon? What's that? 20-some miles?"

"26.2," I answered. "And yes."

"I don't even like to drive that far in a car," he replied with a laugh. "Plus, I'm like you were – a few pounds overweight." He chuckled again as he framed his stomach with his hands, "haven't run a mile since high school."

"You know, most of our athletes are beginners, never attempted anything like this before. They come to the Team for their own reasons – many with a cancer connection, many without. Some start the season without a known connection, and they learn throughout training just how connected they and we all really are to cancer. Some of our athletes just want to do something good for themselves and accomplish a feat others might consider impossible. Whatever the reason, seeing that transformation week-after-week – from 'Can I really do this?' to 'I am doing this' to 'How well am I going to do' – is exhilarating. We coaches get to be part of that transformation season after season – from those first encouraging emails and the season's first miles – all the way to the finish line."

----- **Original Message** -----
From: Your Team In Training Coaches
Hey Team,

Just wanted to wish you all good luck as we embark on "first miles" today.

As your marathon coaches, we believe we have one of the most important jobs in the world: We're in charge of helping you achieve something remarkable – something a lot of people think is impossible. We take that responsibility very seriously, and we're going to take good care of you.

Soak up the experience ahead and know that you all are embarking on something remarkable.

Thanks again for signing on with us. We are in business!

Go Team!

Coaches' Inbox:
First Miles

Coaches,

Thanks for the note. I can't believe training is already here!

I can run several miles straight, but I think I should switch to a run/walk plan. The only problem is – I just give up on myself if I walk too soon. What do you recommend?

Hey there,

Coach here – thanks for getting in touch!

In light of your note, I was really struck by a line in a movie I was watching last night – "Extremely Loud & Incredibly Close." A boy is setting out on a journey of sorts, and he says to us, the audience, **"I decided nothing was going to stop me – not even me."**

Sometimes (many times), we can be our own worst enemy when it comes to ambitious tasks, this notion of "giving up on ourselves."

You know yourself much better than I do, but I know, in my bones, something about you that you may not fully appreciate: If you stick with your training, you will cross that finish line in San Francisco – 26.2 miles. **In about 20-weeks, you will be a marathoner.**

We've got a lot of work to do between now and then, and the first thing we need to do is eliminate "giving up" as an option. It is not an option on race day; it is no longer an option during our training runs (barring actual injury). If you set out for 2 miles – or 26.2 miles – your mindset needs to be, "I am going to finish my assignment – run, walk or crawl." (And if you want to finish faster, you'll be doing more running/walking – than crawling.) Do not give yourself the out of "If I walk now, I'm going to quit. That's just what I do."

Not anymore.

You are training to be an endurance athlete – and we keep moving forward, through sweat, through fatigue, through normal discomfort – **we keep moving forward**. One day at time. One mile at a time.

You can do this – and if you truly believe that – you will.

Athlete's Journey:
Katie Sullivan Poppert's Story – Part II

A bit frustrated by her initial attempts at fundraising, Katie figured she better hit the pavement. First though, she would need new walking shoes, shorts, jog bras, very unnecessary but very cute tops, a Nike sports chip, a sports fanny pack for water...

"I might hurt like hell out there, but, dammit, I was going to *look* good," she said. "And so what if I spent more money than I had earned for the cause so far. Ultimately, it was all for the cause anyway, right?"

She grabbed her dog Frisco's leash, very carefully placed her Nike chip that tracked pace, distance and time, strapped on her fanny pack, attached her phone and iPod, laced up her new shoes and hit the road.

"That first day, I was MOVING," she recalled. "I mean, I had never walked so fast or with such effort in my life. The key was to try and move quickly without looking like too much of a dork. I just couldn't do the whole 'wogging' arm swing thing, but I was anxious to get it over with as quickly as possible without actually jogging. Frisco, naturally, was pulling on his leash so hard that I was sure my right arm would be two inches longer by the time we got home. And every leaf, every bug, needed to be investigated along the way. Maybe training with him wasn't such a great idea after all..."

Katie decided to just go four miles that first day out. As she turned around at mile two to head home, she was feeling pretty good. Pretty proud of herself. She was rocking out to her iPod, enjoying the beautiful day, and putting one foot in front of the other. Then her hip started to swell.

"This was an all too familiar sensation to me, and one that I was really hoping to avoid, at least until I was able to conquer more mileage! My left leg began to lose its swing as the swelling increased, and I began to have an awkward limp."

Still moving quickly, she was now visibly limping.

"So much for not looking like a dork. I was even having to pull my out-of-shape dog along during that last never-ending mile," she said.

Then, just as she was about to throw in the towel, a silver, convertible VW bug pulled out in front of her. Christy drives a silver convertible VW bug.

"It wasn't her, but it was just the motivation I needed," she said "There was a reason I was doing this, a reason that I loved dearly. And I could handle the swelling."

Back home, as she gulped down ibuprofen and sank, exhausted, into the chair in her home office, she realized that this was bigger than just her and her aching pelvis. This was about people suffering, truly suffering, with blood cancers. This was about all the people who surround those patients, who love them and ache for them and pray daily for their recovery. Katie would never get the chance to know her brother-in-law. She had been forced to say goodbye to her friend, Jeff. She had seen countless people have to face the reality of an early death on the oncology floor. She had been with her best friend every day during her frightening ordeal.

"And if I could make a difference, even a little bit of a difference, by raising money to promote research, then I would do whatever it took. I would endure whatever I needed to. But first, I had to invest in some serious ibuprofen."

----- Original Message -----
From: Your Team In Training Coaches

Hey Team,

Never forget, the change you are making in your lives is real.

The inspiration you are offering those around you is real.

The hope you are giving to those living in the shadow of a cancer diagnosis is real.

I know we've just met, but we can say this with certainly – you are all remarkable people, willing to face a daunting challenge head on – 26.2 miles? 13.1 miles? Cancer?

During our time together, we will not let you forget that.

Athlete Reflections:
"We Never Train Alone."
– Phil Ham, TNT athlete

Prior to his introduction to TNT and LLS (at age 61) and during the nearly 20 years preceding his involvement, Phil admits he could have been a poster boy for the inactive life of a couch potato. While he was highly active in sports and athletics from junior high through college, a bout with colon cancer at age 40 put the squelch on most of that activity. (At least that is where he lay the blame for the "miserable condition" of his body and mind.)

One day, he took a look in the mirror and, not liking what he saw, started on a treadmill. The boredom of it all inspired him to blow the dust off an old bike and start riding again.

"For some reason, and I will give credit where credit is due, the Lord introduced me to the concept of a triathlon, and I began training for the 2004 James O'Rourke Triathlon in North Platte, Neb.," Phil recalled.

Beforehand, while sitting and waiting for his turn in the pool, Phil noticed a lot of athletes in purple – and they had some similarly-clad people cheering them on with great enthusiasm. They were athletes with Team In Training, a program Phil inquired about and decided he could "get into."

"I decided to take a shot at the 2005 Seagull Century Ride in Maryland, a fall event – and I was immediately struck by the enormity of the task of raising $5000. I had never done anything like it before," he said.

Once again, he gave up his insecurity to the Lord and decided that if it was His will for Phil to make to his goal, he would do so.

"Clearly, He expected me to do my part. With guidance from the helpful folks at Team, and a lot of friends and family making considerable donations, I was able to meet and exceed my goal," Phil said.

As for the training required for a former coach potato to be able to ride 100 miles? Phil described it as "extensive and fun."

"Since I live far enough from the Omaha/Lincoln area where most of my teammates were located, I was pretty much on my own. I must tell you, however, that I never once rode by myself," Phil said. "To the disinterested onlooker, I was alone, but to a Believer, I always had a constant companion, the same One whose guidance I seek daily and to whom I owe my very being."

He added, "As I continued to train, my body and mind responded so that I found myself in what can only be described as a life-saving condition. The many weeks of riding four and five times a week paid great dividends and continue to do so even now."

The culmination of the training was a spectacular ride through the streets and country side of Maryland during which not even five-and-a-half inches of rain in six-and-a-half hours in the saddle could dampen Phil's spirits.

"With the same loving guidance and support from TEAM, I have run a marathon, a couple of half marathons, completed numerous triathlons, an endurance duathlon, and three century rides. And, at age 68, I plan on at least one more season and two more events."

Phil's goal is to become the first triple, Triple Crown winner in Nebraska with the knowledge that the real winners, because of his involvement, "are the many victims of leukemia and lymphoma whose lives might be spared because of the money I have helped raise.

"I am just one of hundreds of thousands athletes – young and old – who have participated with TEAM and I can't speak for each and every one of them. I can say, however, that my experience with TEAM was truly life changing," he said. "The incredible people I have met, trained with, laughed and cried with have enriched my life beyond my wildest dreams."

The Battle against Cancer: On the Front lines

Dr. Tim Dunnigan, clinical psychologist, on the psychology of cancer

What does a patient go through psychologically at diagnosis? What does the family go through?
Both the patient and family, initially, often experience the same reactions. They find it hard to believe and question whether the diagnosis is correct. The overwhelming emotions of permanent loss of family or loved one make this quite reasonable. All the plans and hopes for the future are now in doubt or lost. All the accommodations and routines that allow people to deal with life are now in jeopardy: Who will pick-up the children? Pay the bills? Earn the money? Make dinner?

With time and further testing, most come to accept the reality of the disease and, when helped with a strong support system, begin to see ways to adjust to this new reality of severe illness, disability, and, perhaps, death.

A critical psychological issue for a person diagnosed with a life-threatening or terminal disease is the support he or she experiences. A person who is surrounded by loved family members or close friends – people who work together to assume responsibilities for him or her and who are available to share intimate feelings about facing the end of life – is most likely to maintain a sense of emotional wholeness. This allows the ill person to call on many and avoid feeling he or she has burdened one person with too much.

Where do people gain strength from?
There are individuals who are simply emotionally strong. They are resilient to stress, can experience a wide range of emotions, and maintain a healthy sense of self in the most extreme circumstance. These fortunate people usually gain this from a lifetime of support, nurturing and success in difficult circumstances. Others draw their support from those who surround them. One sees this particularly in children who can only be as strong as their primary caregivers. Some draw their strength from their faith or philosophy of life. This can give a person a sense of place in the world, even after death. It can give a family a sense of unity at a time when all might fear isolation.

How does a program like Team In Training help or give hope?
I'd like to use my personal experience to answer this question.

In 2003, my wife, Donna, a long-time Team In Training participant and mentor, became ill. She was quite fit having just mentored the Rock 'n' Roll Marathon in San Diego. She began to experience anxiety, confusion, vague pains and balance problems. In a short time, these worsened, and she was diagnosed with primary central nervous system lymphoma.

Prior to treatment, she fell and fractured a number of vertebrae, so treatment was delayed to allow her to recover. Shortly after her first chemotherapy treatment, she contracted a Methicillin-resistant staph infection. This spread rapidly throughout her system, including into her spine through the fractures. She spent days in intensive care. When she began to recover, she couldn't walk, and she couldn't sit upright without putting on an acrylic shell that encompassed her chest from neck-to-waist in order to support her spine. It was terribly hot.

Donna was receiving great physical therapy, learning to take two to three steps while holding railings with both hands. She was told to walk every day, even if only a few steps. This was both physically painful and emotionally overwhelming for a woman who was accustomed to excellent health and ability. She resisted her exercises, asking to do them later or cut them short. She was struggling with the urge to give-up.

One day, one of Donna's TNT coaches, Cheryl, came with Donna's Team In Training jacket. We got the back brace on and the jacket over it, and Cheryl took Donna by the arm and walked with her. It was a touching moment of love for us all. Cheryl gave Donna the hope of regaining her mobility by reminding her of the marathon training that Donna experienced and helped others achieve. Other Team In Training participants began to visit, some who never knew Donna, to encourage her. Others still brought me and my family much appreciated dinners.

By June of 2004, Donna had lived in the hospital about half the previous year. She was improving, but still facing a few more chemotherapy sessions. Her chemotherapy required her to be hospitalized and had numerous and severe side-effects. Infections remained a fear.

Just before the Rock 'n' Roll Marathon, some Team In Training participants brought her a large "Go Team!" banner. (She happened to be in a hospital room overlooking the hill on I-163 where the race descends to Mission Valley.) With her nurse's help, they put the banner in her window. The next Sunday, we pushed her bed to the window and raised it so she could look down on the runners and walkers streaming by. She spent much of the morning watching to see participants wave up at her and the banner. She saw a number do so and was delighted.

Donna finished her treatments and was declared in remission. Less than six weeks later, her symptoms returned and the lymphoma raged-through her brain. She tried one more round of chemotherapy, but this time it had no effect on the lymphoma.

In the last few weeks of her life, while she was dying in hospice, one of her mentees, a man who had overcome a severe head injury by participating in TNT, visited her and told her how important she had been in his life. She had helped him get to training sessions as he could not remember routes or locations, even with written notes. This was another way that she realized her life had meaning and purpose, even as she knew it was ending. She died in September of 2004.

We had great support through Donna's disease. All my family helped. Friends came to San Diego for weeks to sit with her and help me. Her physicians and nurses were terrific and loved Donna for her positive attitude and patience. Our friends from Team In Training were an important source of love and help.

Five

GROUP TRAINING

"Very, very quickly, my teammates became my friends – and remain so."
– Art Herman, TNT athlete/mentor

"By the end of the season, I had more friends, mentors, and coaches than I ever thought I would have in my life." **– Shambra L. Clifford, TNT athlete**

"And your Team trains together, I assume? For accountability and such?" my fellow traveler asked.

"Group training," I said, sipping the last of my plastic-cupped water ration. "Absolutely. It is a vital part of the Team In Training experience – what puts the TEAM in Team In Training."

----- **Original Message** -----
From: Your Team In Training Coaches
Hey Team,

What a tremendous turnout for your first group training session today! Thanks to all who came out. A pleasure seeing so many of you – phenomenal! This is a dedicated, enthusiastic crew!

You've logged your first miles with us, spilled your first drops of sweat. You're in it now & we couldn't be happier to have you.

We've told some of you that group training is for your benefit not ours.

We lied.

Group training raises us up every week and fills us with positive energy. It is so inspiring to be in the company of people who are not only determined to improve themselves but also the world around them. It's going to be a remarkable few months for all of us!

Go Team!

"Saturday morning after Saturday morning," I explained, "we run our longest miles of the week together – and that's when strangers become teammates, teammates become friends and coaches become confidantes. Chafing? Stomach issues? We talk about it all. You know you've arrived as a coach when you open your inbox to find a picture of a blood and pus filled blister – dubbed Elvis – and a note that reads, 'My career as a foot model is officially sunk.'"

My row-mate threw me a polite chuckle, tinged with a dash of disgust. My bad. I quickly changed the subject; non-runners don't want to hear about our blisters and black toenails (as much as runners want to talk about them...).

I continued, "We get the job done week after week, but, in Omaha at least, we are a laid back group. No barking at anyone to 'Get those knees up!' or 'Get the lead out!' Any concern about attending group training usually melts away after one session. And before long, our athletes actually come to crave that Team time – every Saturday morning, rain or shine (unless there is lightning, ice cover, or temps below 10 degrees)."

We woke this morning to 4" of snow and 9 miles to run. We suited up in our armor and headed out on our laps around 'Lake Z.' We were actually cutting a path around most of our first lap. Very pretty and really cool.

Everything was fine until we were just about done. The ground had started melting back the snow, and we found ourselves running in slush. You would take a step and splash ice water into your opposite shoe... This was about the worst I have been through yet and will do all I can to avoid this whenever possible. All in all though, it was a great experience for us. – **Scott J. McCoid, TNT athlete (from his training blog)**

"There is camaraderie at group training," I told my row-mate, "the joy of a shared purpose and the comfort of shared pain – physical and emotional. Remember, most TNT athletes come from a place of cancer-driven pain. Group training for some, group therapy for others."

**Athlete's Journey:
Art Herman's Story – Part I**

Art's wife Linda was diagnosed in January 2002 with indolent small B cell non-Hodgkin's lymphoma, a very slow growing type of cancer that eventually transforms into an aggressive cancer. Until then, you lead a perfectly normal life, except for periodic visits with the oncologist and your own knowledge of the disease's traditional progression.

Art first became aware of Team In Training at the 2003 the San Diego Rock 'n' Roll Marathon. He was running on his own – but couldn't help notice all the purple-clad runners being cheered on by large groups of very supportive people.

Ironically, it was Linda who talked him *out* of joining TNT in 2003. She said she didn't know how much time she had and wanted to share as much of that time with him... And so they did.

The cancer transformed in May 2008, and after many different treatments, Linda passed away on June 6, 2009.

Art joined TNT mid-season in July 2009.

"To say I was emotionally raw would be an understatement, but I'm not a procrastinator. I knew that I needed to do something. I wanted to vent in a healthy, constructive way, and this seemed like the perfect fit. However, I didn't know anyone associated with TNT. I had no idea what the people would be like, or if I was even ready to take this on. I only knew that I would give it my best shot and see what happened," Art recalled.

At his very first group training session, Art met his mentor, Laurie Houston, who introduced him to Coach Cheryl Sheremeta and Asst. Coach Dave Marinkovich.

"Everyone was so upbeat and positive and genuine that I immediately began to feel comfortable," he said.

He later found himself running with another participant, Christine Balderas. She introduced herself and then proceeded to ask what brought him to the group. As Art was sharing his story, he could see tears streaming down her face.

"Very, very quickly, my teammates became my friends and remain so," Art said. "What I found out about TNT, is that the quality of the people you meet, whether staff or participant, is off the charts. I guess when you think about it, it really shouldn't be a surprise. We are all like-minded, in that we are ready to give our time and effort to this great cause, and that we have taken the huge step that separates thought from action."

Athlete's Journey:
Shambra L. Clifford's Story – Part II

"I've always had a hard time making friends, and I didn't have many in San Diego when I joined Team In Training," Shambra recalled. "During the training sessions, you can almost always find someone who runs at your pace. It's then that you start connecting with them in so many ways. You learn their stories, their strengths and weakness, their personalities, and even their jokes. Running those long miles almost forces you to get to know the people you are running with.

"We were always there to offer advice to one another and to keep each other motivated. By the end of the season, I had more friends, mentors, and coaches than I ever thought I would have in my life. You create amazing bonds with everyone. You share the same passion for endurance sports and for helping others. I started Team In Training with a goal, but I ended it with so much more."

"What about someone like me?" my fellow traveler asked. "I wouldn't be able to keep up with a group."

"That's the beauty of it. You don't have to," I answered. "You don't have to run or walk any faster or slower than you want to. Since we have such a fabulous spectrum of athletes, odds are someone is going to match your pace. As for your coaches, it's our job to meet you where you are – not the other way around."

I added for emphasis, "We know there's going to be some hesitation: How does the formal training work? Do we run in a pack? What if I'm not as fast as everyone else? Common questions among our beginner athletes – and we diffuse them every season."

Coaches' Inbox:
Group Training

Hi Coach,

I am looking forward to meeting you and the team on Saturday, however I don't believe I am at their ability level. I will come anyway and can just do my miles by myself so I don't hold anyone back.

Hey there,

Coach here – You are dedicated and courageous, and I want you to stop worrying about how you stack up compared to other members of the team, stop worrying about holding others back.

Training with the group is going to be great for you because you'll see you're right in line with the bulk of the team. Yes, we train together, but we train at our own paces. If someone's faster, they'll push ahead. If someone's a bit slower, they'll fall back. No big deal, that's how it works.

Bottom line: We have people of all degrees of ability on the team. That's what's so great about this. I'd say 95% of your teammates are beginners, going farther than they've ever gone before.

Athlete Reflections:
"I Could Not Have Been More Wrong."
– Mackenzie Raber, TNT athlete

The initial concept of team runs bright and early on Saturday mornings seemed daunting. Mackenzie thought she was throwing herself into a group of running gurus that would leave her in the dust, reminding her of all the reasons she initially thought she was unfit to attempt a full marathon.

"I could not have been more wrong," she said. "The eager faces at Lake Z – our weekly team training spot – were not only calming but motivating as we stepped off for each run and gradually saw our weekly miles increase. These were the same faces that I saw shed tears at the pre-race Inspiration Dinner, the same faces that were overjoyed and filled with smiles post-race as we all reveled in the individual goals we just accomplished."

As we were coming up on the two mile point this morning, I caught up to a teammate who I hadn't seen at training before. She was running alone and was struggling, hurting. I paced with her for a while and found out this was her "first time running." I talked with her about a few of the strategies we had been taught to make things go a little easier – and she went on to finish her first 4.5 miler!

Here is the cool part: Here I am, a first timer myself, able to help another. We all have different paths, and we need to realize there are people all around us that we can lean on when the going gets tough, no matter who or where we are. There are times when you need to be carried and those other times when you can be the one to carry others. **– Scott J. McCoid, TNT athlete (from his training blog)**

----- Original Message -----
From: Your Team In Training Coaches
"Two are better than one because they have a good return for their labor. For if either of them falls, the one will lift up his companion. But woe to the one who falls when there is not another to lift him up." – Ecclesiastes 4:9-10.

Remember Team, though we may train by ourselves sometimes, we never train alone.

You are all part of an amazing group, a team of like-minded individuals sharing the same goals and concerns. Relish this experience, lift each other up. And, as you lift each other up, know that you're lifting us up as well. It is, as always, our profound privilege and pleasure to "in training" with you.

Go Team!

Athlete Reflections:
"Because I Can"
– Angie Dougherty, TNT athlete/mentor

Angie first joined Team In Training in 2008 after her dad was diagnosed with throat cancer. In December of 2009, after three months of five-day-a-week radiation, he was given a clean bill of health. (The doctor actually told him he looked better than ever!)

Then, on March 19, 2010, Angie received the call. The cancer was back – everywhere – and terminal. Her Dad. Her hero. Her world from the age of 3 to 21 as he raised Angie and her brother as a single parent.

"There was nothing they could do, but I knew there was something I could do. I immediately called LLS to sign up for whatever event was next (the Nike Women's Marathon in San Francisco) and started fundraising," Angie said.

While training at the lake one Saturday, about two miles into a 4-mile run, Angie found herself running with a new teammate, Adrianne.

"Being alumni and a mentor, I was always prying information out of the 'newbies.' Adrianne told me she was running for her cousin, Drew, who had cancer as a kid. When I told her that I was running for my Dad, she told me her dad was also battling cancer – pancreatic cancer. I was completely shocked that, while here I was going on and on about my dad, her dad was in the same situation," Angie said.

As they talked more, Angie learned that she and Adrianne had a lot in common. Among other things, they'd taken the same boy to homecoming a couple of years apart and Adrianne worked closely with Angie's aunt.

"As the training season went on, I looked forward to running with Adrianne at training and talking about nothing – and everything -- through 13, 15, 18 mile runs! (Though I did learn really quick not to speak a word to Adrianne until she was 3-4 miles into the run.)"

On June 23, 2010, Angie's Dad lost his battle with cancer.

"I did what I know and went to group training that next Saturday. Coach Kelly was the first to approach me. She hugged me and we cried together. She asked, 'What are you doing here?' And I told her, 'This is what I know. You guys are my rock, and I need to be here.' Between the coaches, staff and my teammates, I had the best support out there."

Angie noticed Adrianne was gone – and she hadn't been there the week before either. Busy, she thought. The next week through all the emotion and commotion in her life, Angie learned that Adrianne's dad had lost his battle on the 26th of June.

"There we were," Angie said, "both training for the Nike Women's Marathon. Both having just lost our dads to the disease we are fighting so hard to cure."

She continued, "We found ourselves talking about our emotions from the last few weeks. I'd tell her how hard it was trying to explain it all to my kids. She would tell me about her brother's emotions being different than hers. We would reminisce on the good times we had with our dads. Adrianne's dad had always been a runner so he would encourage her to run. My dad would tell me running a marathon was the dumbest thing he'd ever heard and that I was going to kill myself!

"It was extremely therapeutic to be pounding out 15 or 17 mile runs with someone who's in the same place as you and can relate. Those runs are some of my very favorite memories and are times that helped me heal my broken heart."

On October 15, 2010, Angie, Adrianne and the rest of the Nebraska team traveled to San Francisco for race weekend. Adrianne brought her Mom. During the inspiration dinner, pictures of everyone's honored heroes, including Adrianne's Dad, flashed on the big screen.

"It was an extremely emotional, precious time for Adrianne and her Mom. I was happy to have gotten pictures of them together during that exact moment," Angie recalled.

On October 17th, they ran.

"There were about seven or eight of us who all started out together, and the plan was to stick together 'til the end. Well, in 26 miles you eventually lose someone somewhere!" Angie said.

She and Adrianne got separated – but around mile seven, they found each other again.

"From there on, we ran and walked together," she recalled. "We talked the entire time. We encouraged each other when the pains set in. Adrianne went to school in San Francisco so she knew where we were and where we were going. It was like my personal tour guide running with me! In the end, we finished our 26.2 mile journey, soaking wet from a downpour, on the beach, hand-in-hand. We cried together as we accomplished this huge goal and remembered why we run. That's a popular question. Why do you continue putting yourself through the torture of running a marathon? Because it's very therapeutic – and I can!"

----- Original Message -----
From: Your Team In Training Coaches
Alright Team,
Never forget, it's easy to be a "could" person.
I could do this if I felt like it; I could do that if I had the time.
No consequence, no sacrifice, no reward.
You all have made the leap to "will" people.

I will train for an endurance event; I will fundraise thousands of dollars; I will venture

beyond my comfort zone and push myself to the limits.

It is your 'wills' that have already allowed you to accomplish such tremendous things.

It is your 'wills' that will propel you to the finish line on race day.

It is your 'wills' that continue to inspire us day-after-day.

Team In Training Spotlight:
Any Given Saturday
– A Coaches' Perspective on Group Training

6:02 a.m., Lake Zorinsky, southwest Omaha

Clink... clink... clink...

The sound breaks the quiet of a refreshingly cool August morning. A volunteer, wearing a bright green shirt and wielding a mallet, drives a spike into the ground. The pole tent canopy he's anchoring is one of several in a makeshift "race village." Maybe "his" canopy will serve as the registration area or a venue for post-race massage or, if it's lucky, the coveted finisher's oasis promising cookies, bottled water and, if fortune is smiling on the participants, some kind of ice cream treat.

Fellow volunteers, also clad in bright green, execute their orders, loading boxes of bananas, sleeves of plastic cups, and full water coolers onto the beds of idling golf carts. They'll be dispatched shortly to set up aid stations along the course.

A finish line crew erects the official time clock, its digital red numbers spinning down to the official start time – one hour and 58 minutes to go...

Coffee is in plentiful supply. It's early.

I observe the pre-race scurry from a distance. I am not – nor do I have athletes – participating in this particular race, "Strides for Education," a 10K, 5K or fun half-mile run/walk to support a local school district. In Omaha, spring through fall, you can count on a race just about every weekend, supporting one good cause or another. Make-a-Wish. Juvenile Diabetes. Cancer.

In one hour and 57 minutes, hundreds of people – young, older, fit and not-so-much – will gather at the starting line, absorb the pre-race excitement flowing through the crowd, and feel the jolt in their gut when that gun goes off.

Big or small, I love race mornings.

Still, I set off on my own for now, leaving the scurry of preparation behind, determined to get in a couple of "warm up miles" before our athletes arrive for regular Saturday group training at 6:30 a.m.

The morning sky is streaked with those heavenly reds and oranges, the sun just making its climb. In the distance, two running silhouettes make their way across the dam – the "damn dam" as some have taken to calling it. (A fitting designation in the dead of winter when a brutal Nebraska headwind threatens to freeze the goo in your eyes and that unshielded concrete span – that damn dam – just seems to go on forever...) A haze of mist floats off the lake, hovering in the calm. Peace.

The alarm clock had shrieked – as it does every Saturday morning – like a demon at 5:20 a.m. Instantaneously and inevitably, the unforgiving blare was followed by a moment of sheer confusion.

"Who? Wha-zah?"

As I came to my senses, it all started to make sense – Saturday. Group training. Can't be late. I grudgingly pulled myself out of bed. Enthusiasm would come soon – it always does. But, at the moment, I was just tired.

I brushed my teeth, slathered my pits with Right Guard and popped in my contacts, pulled on my purple TNT training shirt and affixed my well-worn, black running hat. My smelly black hat. How many miles have we run together old friend in how many places? Too many to count.

The routine has become wonderfully robotic – put a fresh sign-in sheet on the red clipboard, fill the trusty blue water jugs and place them at strategic points along the day's route.

Somewhere between my house and the lake, my car largely alone on the sleepy streets, that rush of excitement will hit. Our athletes are going to gather in a few minutes; they're going to push themselves;

they're going to accomplish. Some will run, walk or run/walk farther than they've ever gone before. Today. Before most people have even started their days.

6:11 a.m., Lake Zorinsky, southwest Omaha

The cool air embraces me this August morning, a sheer delight after a brutal Omaha summer. I hope the crisp mornings are here to stay. Either way, I'm making the most of this one. The trail is largely empty at this hour. But, I know my athletes are on the way and that pushes me. 13 miles on the schedule today for our marathoners-in-training; 5 miles for our half marathoners-in-training. I hit the one mile marker, pull up, turn-around, walk, stretch out my shins, and start heading back. The "first mile" aches – crunchy knees, a little calf twinge – dissipated quicker than usual today. It's going to be a good day.

I finish my warm-up with a few minutes to spare – 6:25 a.m. The Strides for Education race begins in about 90 minutes, and the pre-race scurry continues. Headlights approach in the distance, the TNT cavalry, I hope. Indeed, as the cars park and the occupants emerge, I see that these are "my" people.

As they emerge from their cars, sleepy-eyed, fidgeting with their iPods and fuel belts, their sacrifice is not lost on me. They've given up their comfortable beds, their leisurely Saturday mornings, their seats in the bleachers at their kids' early morning soccer or baseball games. Their reward, this morning, is a live view of the sunrise, a metaphor, as I see it, for the entire season. You can't witness the sunrise if you don't sacrifice some sleep. You can't reap the rewards of race day if you don't sacrifice your time, your effort, your body... These are not ordinary people gathering to run and walk; they are extraordinary.

We make small talk. I explain the route (for you marathoners, three laps around the eastern half of the lake today...) and touch on a couple of training tips. Then, we huddle. (As a child, I didn't do a lot of team sports, so the huddle, to me, is a very special, better-late-than-never component of group training.) Everyone puts their hands in the center, and we bring it back to the mission, even if just for a brief few minutes.

"Who are we training for today? Just shout it out," I say.

"My brother."

"My nephew."

"My best friend from college."

"My son's teacher."

"My cousin who was just diagnosed."

The list goes on. That's why we are here. That's why we give up those comfy beds and those leisurely Saturday mornings – because the list goes on.

"Go Team on three," I bark. "One, two, three…"

It's time to go to work.

"GO TEAM!"

----- Original Message -----
From: Your Team In Training Coaches
Alright Team,

We mentioned it early on in the season and we'll mention it again: This is the real deal, a bona fide test of the human spirit, proof that steady determination can tame the "impossible" and silence the naysayers.

You all made a remarkable choice months ago. You looked at the training schedule and the fundraising requirements, and you said, "Not only can I do this, I WILL do this. I will give of my time; I will give of my body and I will not back down until I have crossed that finish line."

Being a spectator is easy. It takes courage to get in the ring, to push harder and endure longer than our bodies might prefer. Keep pushing, Team. You are cresting that hill changed people, and we are so proud of you for what you've achieved – for yourselves, for others. And, we'll let you in on a little secret: You've already accomplished the amazing. Race day is simply your rewards for a job well done – and what a reward it will be!

Go Team!

Six

MEETING THE HONORED HERO

°*"As a Mom, I cannot put into words how absolutely awful it is to watch your baby girl endure such harsh treatment. No person, especially a child, should have to go through this. My mission is to move mountains until we find a CURE for Lily – and for everyone! That's why I have joined Team In Training."* **– Susie Dotson, TNT athlete/mother of honored hero**

"I told you I was familiar with the Leukemia & Lymphoma Society," my row-mate said as we pushed toward San Diego.

"Right," I replied.

"It goes deeper than that," he volunteered. "My wife and I actually lost our daughter to AML about six years ago." (Acute myeloid leukemia (AML) – a cancer of the bone marrow and the blood that progresses quickly without treatment.)

"I'm so sorry to hear that," I said. Sincerely.

"After she was diagnosed, we joined an LLS family support group and received just a ton of information from the Society about Cheryl's disease and the different clinical trials. We didn't need the financial aid piece, thanks goodness, but it was reassuring to know it was there," he said.

"Cheryl is your daughter," I said. "I'm sorry, all this time, I never asked your name."

"I'm Richard," he said, extending his hand.

"Dan," I said as we shook.

"Dan," he repeated. "Nice to meet you."

"How old was Cheryl when she passed?" I asked.

"She was 27," Richard said. "Had just gotten married two years prior."

He paused. I knew that pause all too well. His eyes welled up with tears. It never gets any easier.

"Cancer," he said.

"Cancer," I repeated.

"I didn't know about Team In Training back then. I wished I would have," he said. "Sounds like it could have been very therapeutic."

"For us, Team in Training has been a life raft," I replied. "Without it, my wife and I could have 'drowned' during some very dark times in our lives – too many cancer diagnoses, too many cancer deaths. Instead, the Team In Training experience is something positive when we've been dealt such negatives. It's our message to cancer that says, 'You've devastated me, but you have not defeated me.'"

Two strangers on a plane connected by the spider web of cancer.

"Cancer is a bully – and it is unrelenting," I added. "Two years after my sister passed away, Kelly's mother was diagnosed with breast cancer. She fought the disease the same way she lived her life – with courage, humor, dignity. We lost her in 2009."

I paused – that pause. "When my times comes to be tested, I hope I can confront my trial with a fraction of the strength that Sharon and my mother-in-law and Cheryl, I'm sure, confronted their trials."

I continued, "It really is very humbling – knowing, without a doubt, that even a six-year-old girl is so much stronger than I am. My daughter's best little friend, Lily, was diagnosed with high risk ALL just three days after celebrating her 5th birthday. Her mother, Susie, had noticed some unusual bruising and took her to the pediatrician to check her iron count…"

Five minutes. That's how long it took the doctor to survey Lily's enlarged liver, spleen and bruises and tell the family that they needed to bring Lily to the hospital right away.

Lily had cancer.

The family sped home to get Lily's favorite doll, packed their bags and essentially moved into Omaha's Children's Hospital & Medical Center for the next 28 days.

Lily's treatment started within 24 hours of her diagnosis. Within a year, she had undergone over a dozen blood and platelet transfusions, 98 leg shots, over a dozen spinal taps and a port surgery. (Her first year chances of beating the cancer were 40 percent. With her 6th birthday, she moved up to 70 percent.) Lily took chemo every day – and completed her treatment in early January 2014.

In sharing Lily's story with the Omaha team, mother Susie wrote, "Lily is an amazing person – still quick to share a smile! She is a true testament to the resiliency of a child."

And, in November 2012, Susie joined the Team herself and, in her daughter's honor, began training for her first marathon.

"As a Mom, I cannot put into words how absolutely awful it is to watch your baby girl endure such harsh treatment. **No person, especially a child, should have to go through this.** My mission is to move mountains until we find a **CURE** for Lily -- and for everyone!

"That's why I have joined **Team In Training (TNT)** -- the Leukemia & Lymphoma Society's key fundraising campaign -- and formed **Lily's Mission Team**! A group of friends and I are raising funds to help find cures and better treatments for leukemia, lymphoma, Hodgkin's disease and myeloma.

"In addition, we're spending the next five months training with TNT to complete a **full marathon** in Lincoln, Neb. I will lift up my **400+ hours of training** to all who suffer from cancer and to those who got their wings early. And, I will keep you all in my heart as we hit the finish line at **26.2 miles!**"

"That's why we do it," I said to this former stranger, this grieving father. "We do it for Lily and the far too many like her who are living in the shadow of this disease. We do it for moms and dads and brothers and sisters. Those who've passed – and those still fighting. These are our honored heroes. Our inspirations."

Every Team is attached to a "teamwide" honored hero, I explained, typically a child such as Lily who the athletes, in addition to their own, personal honored heroes, will raise up and dedicate their training ("If they can endure chemo, we can endure 13.1 or 26.2 miles" – a very common mantra.).

"Many teams also have – and will rally around – their 'honored teammates,' cancer survivors who've come back to settle a score."

A Survivor's Story:
Heartbreak and Triumph: A Pep Talk to the Team
– Ashley True, TNT honored teammate,
in her own words

My first connection to the word "lymphoma" came when I was about three years old, and my Mom, 24 at the time, was diagnosed with Hodgkin's lymphoma.

That was 1984 – and her only treatment option was radiation. (If you know how tough radiation is now, you can imagine how bad it was back then). The radiation brought results, but the doctors warned my mom that cancer may come back – and it did. She was diagnosed with esophageal cancer in Oct. 1996, just days after she turned 37 years old. She passed away a few short months later in Jan. 1997. I was 15 years old.

Six years later – almost to the date – still feeling the after-effects of being hit by the cancer truck, I was hit again. In Jan 2003, at the age of 21, I was diagnosed with Hodgkin's lymphoma, stage IIa. My mom's exact diagnosis.

As some of you survivors know, being diagnosed is not always the scary part; it's when you're finished with treatment that it becomes frightening. Don't get me wrong, being told I had the same cancer as my mom, was going to lose my hair, and may not be able to have children, scared the shit out of me and the rest of my family. But, at that point, I was in the zone, fighting for my life. (There was also a tiny voice inside my head saying, "Well, this isn't a surprise." Weird.)

It wasn't until I'd been in remission for five years, with one scare of reoccurrence behind me, that I really started to lose my mind. You see, no matter how hard you try, life after cancer will never be 'normal' again. Yet, I was trying so hard to fit my old norm – so much so that it was causing major conflict with my emotional self.

This is where the Leukemia & Lymphoma Society (LLS) comes into my story.

After speaking to a few professionals and some family members, we concurred that I wasn't crazy and that this was, actually, normal. They suggested that I get involved in support groups and maybe some non-profits whose sole mission is to cure cancer. It felt great hanging around people who shared my passion for making cancer history as well as people who understood firsthand what being a survivor is like. I started with LLS's Light the Night walk in 2008 and became the honored hero in 2009. Then in 2011, I joined Team In Training.

I signed up to do the Nike Women's Half Marathon in San Francisco during a kick-off event at Soaring Wings Winery just outside of Omaha. (I am not going to blame the wine, but it surely made signing on the dotted line much easier...)

I joined the Team for many reasons:
- I just turned 30 years old
- I'd be fulfilling something remarkable in my life
- I was accepting a challenge I created on my own terms
- The wine

So, I got my new shoes, started my training miles and damn, it felt good! I had never been a runner. I ran track in high school, and by "running track in high school," I mean I attended a few practices and ran the mile once. Just once. That was it. I ran for fun in college three miles here, four miles there, nothing crazy.

My first training run – with my mentor Lisa – I ended up running four miles. Rock star. I thought, "Wow, this is easy… 13.1 may not be a big enough challenge for me."

A few days later, I emailed my coach and said sign me up for the full: "I am going big or going home!" (I referred back to this email several times during my training while yelling, "What the hell was I thinking?!")

Training was tough. The toughest thing I have ever willingly put myself through, but there were so many things and so many people that kept me going. I rested here and there, and cussed a lot, but the vision of crossing that finish line in San Francisco made me go one more mile and then another.

I know they say there is no crying in baseball, but someone forgot to tell them about running. Wow, I never knew running could be so emotional; it really is like therapy in its cheapest form. There were many times, running around Lake Zorinsky and the Papio Trail, when a song would come across my iPod and I would get teary-eyed thinking about how far I've come and what I was running for. It was awesome – but then it got awkward.

People passing me probably thought something was terribly wrong with me. Can you imagine seeing someone running and crying? Running AND crying? And, who puts country music on their iPod? Especially their wedding song? I learned to shuffle pass those songs until I hit some Gaga or Eminem who put me back in my place.

Then, graduation day came. I didn't need country music to make me want to cry that day. 20 miles. I just ran 20 miles! Forget about the fact that I want to pass out and cry. I just ran 20 miles!

I can do this. I will do this.

On October 16, 2011, I did.

I crossed that finish line in San Francisco and received my finisher's jersey, my Tiffany's necklace and whole lotta pride. I just ran for 6 hours and 26 point freaking 2 miles! Rock star! (To be honest, my first thoughts, when I crossed that finish line, were, "Give me some chocolate milk and a bagel, and point me to that ocean. I need my cold soak!") It wasn't until the next day, when I couldn't walk, that I became most proud of myself. I did it.

And if you thought this story couldn't get any better, I am happy to say that my husband and I are expecting our first child in August. The fear of not being able to conceive is far behind me, and I couldn't be more thrilled about my future.

In all seriousness, I hope listening to my crazy little story can give you a little push during those tough days and give you faith in knowing you can do this. Bless you all on this run and the many more to come. You have my thoughts and prayers until you cross that finish line and beyond. Good luck, have fun – and GO TEAM!

Update: Samuel David True arrived 8/22/12 (6 days late) and was 9 lbs 5oz and 22" long. "Big boy, long labor and worth every minute!"

Honored Heroes:
For My Mother Maria – Laura Korkowski, TNT athlete

My Mother Maria Elisabeth Kayhart was my best friend, the woman who was friends with everyone, a bright spot in every room, the mom who every kid wanted to have as their mom. She had such a zest for life, and it was unreal when she was diagnosed with multiple myeloma at age 56.

I remember the phone call like it was yesterday. It was the same day that I got engaged. I called, so excited to tell her my big news; she was picking up the phone to tell me hers.

We learned that multiple myeloma was a very new form of cancer, tended to affect older men and had no cure. Mom immediately spent months trying to find a specialist who she felt comfortable with. She fell in love with her doctor, Dr. Seigel, who was always on the cutting edge of the new treatments. They harvested stem cells and started her on chemo and radiation. Never once did Mom walk into that office without a smile. The nurses loved to see her, the other patients loved to see her, her doctor loved to see her. She always thought of others, knowing which of the nurses was going to get married, graduate, move or have a baby.

When the stem cell transplant only triggered a short remission period, the experimental treatments started. Never once did Mom say no. Never once did she show how tired she actually was to those around her.

Her drive and determination got her to dance at my wedding and got me though my divorce nine months later. (I should have listened to her...).

She got to see my brother graduate college and buy his first house.

She got to see my sister grow in business and take her company by storm.

She got to dance at my second wedding.

It was about five years into treatment that I realized all these experimental procedures, even though they were not knocking her into remission, were keeping her hope alive. It was then that my best friend told me about Team In Training. In my first fundraising effort, I raised over $15,000 (as if you needed more proof to show how much my Mom was loved). People wanted to show her how proud they were of her and her continuous fight.

The Disney Marathon in January 2008 was amazing. All during the race, cheers of "Go Team!" carried me, my purple jersey covered in pictures of my Mother. I knew she was going to be there at the finish line, wearing my silly bachelorette hat so I could find her.

As I rounded the turn and passed the sign for mile 26, there she was. My sister managed to get her on the course, on the divider separating the runners for the finish. I thought I was hallucinating. Her weak little legs stood up from her wheel chair – and she started clapping for me. She sat, and I pushed her that last 0.2 across the line. The memory still makes me cry.

Mom wore my medal for weeks, even slept with it on, and was so proud to show it off to everyone she knew. I would run a marathon every day to get her to smile like that!

After that race, I could tell Mom was running a little low on hope. Six experimental treatments completed and nothing yet to send her cancer back. I found out in May 2008 that I was pregnant, the first grandbaby, a son. Again, Mom put her head down and fought. She got to hold Alex that February day in 2009. She helped me give him his first bath, cut his nails, dress him up and rock him to sleep. She held on to him as long as she could.

That August 2009, she passed away with a picture of him in her hands. Eight years of fighting, eight experimental treatments and two stem cell transplants. She did all that she could, I could not have asked her to fight anymore.

Here we are almost two years later, and I now have a daughter that shares her name. My little girl reminds me of my mother, not only in spirit, but in her smile. I have a small piece of her with me. Chicago 2010 is my first race back since that Disney Marathon day. I know that Mom is not going to be there at mile marker 26. Instead, she will be on my shoulder my entire four hour journey. I cannot wait to get out there for her again.

Boy, do I miss her.

We got some bad news last week though that puts everything we are doing back in perspective. My parents' neighbor and 30-year+ family friend was just diagnosed with lung cancer. And, I just found out that another family friend from Idaho was diagnosed with lymphoma. She's about 30 years old! Cancer sucks! And it doesn't care who you are and what you do when it picks its next victim.

It refocused me on what we are doing, and all that you are doing, to help fund the battles to find the cures. Every single commitment you make brings us one step closer to those goals and again I'd like to say thank you. **- Scott J. McCoid, TNT athlete (from his training blog)**

Honored Heroes:
For My Husband Mike – Judy Mansisidor, TNT athlete

The expletives exploded: "&%*@#$! The jet's on fire! The jet's on fire!"

"Chewy" and "Bee" were flying at 3,000 feet – and 300 mph – in a US Navy S-3 Viking jet, a floating gas station also known as "the Hoover" in reference to the specific noise it made upon landing.

Having forgotten to "safe the mic," Bee, the pilot, continued his litany of expletives for a wide audience to hear, including other aircraft, those in the carrier tower, the captain...

Chewy, the 6'4", hairy (think "Chewbacca") navigator, went to the back of the jet and grabbed the fire extinguisher with his giant hands. The fire was out in seconds.

Once they'd dumped their fuel and landed safely on the deck of the carrier, the commander of the squadron, call sign "Deuce" (earned because he had "splashed" not one, but two jets into the ocean during his career as an aviator), proceeded to chew Bee and Chewy out for not following the EPs (emergency procedures).

Fast forward ten years:

I've been married to Chewy for nine years and we have three children, ages 3, 5 and 6.

"Is Mike there?"

"Who's calling please?"

"This is the med center, calling to confirm Mike's bone biopsy tomorrow at..."

I froze after she said the word "biopsy."

My Chewy, my husband, bone biopsy, cancer, death, widow at 38, three children, no income, empty place at dinner, sleeping alone, weddings with no father, all this spun in my head in seconds.

I simultaneously could not breathe and wanted to throw up. I had to try three times to dial my friend's number. I couldn't get the breath to speak to her to tell her what was up.

"Judy, are you Ok? What is it? What's wrong?!"

Still, I couldn't speak.

"Meet me at the park. I'm on my way now," she said.

I, honestly, don't know how I got myself and my three-year son old, "mini-Chewy," to the park that day. It is half a mile from my house. I know my son didn't drive us. All I remember is standing in the middle of the park, paralyzed with fear. I snapped out of it when my friend, Jennifer, grabbed my shoulders and shook me: "Judy! Judy! Stay in the moment! Don't think about what might happen. Just be right here, right now, and one step at a time."

There are no "EPs" for a leukemia diagnosis.

Update: Judy's husband, Mike, responded quickly to treatment for hairy cell leukemia – and is currently in in remission.

Honored Heroes:
For My Husband, Mauri – Mary Ellen Hellerstedt, TNT athlete

Team In Training is about much more than raising money for LLS. To me, it is what I can do to personally fight back against cancer!

Thanksgiving week 2005, my husband, Mauri Booton, was diagnosed with aggressive large B-cell lymphoma. (He had been weak and very tired for months, but we owned a bakery so he wrote it off to hard work, long hours and loving our business.)

Mauri's treatment was inpatient for seven days with round-the-clock chemotherapy. Then, he'd go home for two weeks, and if blood counts allowed, inpatient seven more days for part two of each series. In the first year, due to chemo and complications, he spent 18 weeks inpatient. But, he always maintained an upbeat "get 'er done" attitude.

Mauri lived for four years after his diagnosis. (His mother, Maggie, had died of lymphoma in 1993, at the age of 61. She only lived 11 months after diagnosis. Treatment options were considerably more limited for her than they were 12 years later when Mauri was diagnosed. This made him even more passionate about volunteering, raising money, giving hope and encouragement and giving back.)

In May 2009, Mauri was second runner up for LLS Man of the Year in Iowa. He worked hard at giving hope and inspiration to anyone touched by cancer. His motto was: "Woo-hoo, life is good!" He taught me lots about how precious life is and that there is no promise of tomorrow, so we'd better do the best we can with each and every day.

After a period of remission, Mauri's cancer returned in late 2009, and he died January 17, 2010, at the age of 60. He had started chemotherapy in preparation for a bone marrow transplant, which we were hoping would happen in Omaha, Neb., late winter 2010.

Mauri knew I had an interest in participating in a Team In Training event. When his cancer returned, he helped me put "feet in motion" to get signed up, attend the first meeting and start the training for the San Diego Rock-n-Roll race.

Mauri had planned to be my coach, mentor, cheerleader, fundraising chief and inspiration. He thanked me daily for my efforts and gave me constant encouragement and believed that I actually could accomplish this – many times, more than I did. Unfortunately, he didn't make it to San Diego, but his spirit was with me the whole way and constantly.

Training helped me work through my grief – a process I know will go on forever. From February-June of 2010, the team, my goal, and the loving care of friends and family kept me going. The people who loved us came out of the woodwork with support, caring and dollars. They helped me raise over $51,000 – and get a research grant in Mauri's name.

So you see, for me, this is all about hope, inspiration, supporting and caring for each other and touching people's lives. I am more a believer than ever that you get back way more than you give if you do it with heart and the right spirit. I can't thank enough all the wonderful people who have lifted me up when I could not reach.

Every day is a gift! May you live it fully!

A Survivor's Story:
The Power to Persevere
– Elizabeth Kerans, TNT honored teammate, in her own words

It had been ten years... Ten years since I got the news that tumors were advancing through my body. Hodgkin's lymphoma. I was to be thankful I suppose. The doctors told me my survival rate was 80 percent.

I remembered my oncologist saying that 10 years after treatment, I could consider myself cured. So to celebrate, I decided to raise money for the Leukemia & Lymphoma Society. Oh yeah, and train for – and complete – a marathon.

Making the decision was a milestone. I remember the adrenaline and excitement I had at the first information meeting. I had come a long way since sitting in the doctor's office, sobbing because I was going to lose my coveted, long hair at the age of 18.

Training hit my body like a wrecking ball. Every Saturday morning, I was awake before the first hints of life emerged. It was just me and the team; our feet pounding the concrete as we brought life to the trail.

Left, right, left, right... I could almost hear the crunching of my undisciplined joints, and the futile complaints of my disgruntled muscles. Left, right, left, right, left, right...

As training progressed, I couldn't help but consider the parallels between training for a marathon and going through chemotherapy and radiation. In both instances, my body was beaten, torn, and defeated. As we added mileage, I wondered if I would actually make it. Was I really going to run *that* far? (I did a lot of walking too. But still, it was a long way to go on foot.)

The big day finally came. I wondered, "Has anyone ever died running a marathon? What was my 'survival rate'?" I was told by our great coaches that it was pretty high, so I hid my fear and persevered.

Persevere.

That is all you can do. When I was sick, everyone said, "You are so strong. How did you do it?"

Well, what choice do you have? You can't just give up and say, "Forget life, I'm going to sit down and die now."

During the race I felt the same way. Thoughts raced through my mind as my feet raced through the course: "I'm not going to make it. I need to stop."

When the last 4 miles were approaching, I had slowed to a crawl. I would glance at the curb and think of how appealing it was. I wanted to stop, sit down and give up. But I persevered as I had done 10 years before.

I did not *run* through the finish line, but I finished. At the time, it was less than glorious for me. It wasn't until several days later that it hit me. I had won again. I raised thousands of dollars that would help other cancer patients. Another comparison – when I finished my last treatment, I was sore, bald and not happy. My elation came later... much later.

I still have the shoes that I ran my first marathon in. They are literally stained with blood, sweat and tears. Yes, I said my *first* marathon. Three years later, I decided to do it again, in large part, because I missed the culture of the Team.

You can't explain the level of camaraderie that you have with the team you train with. You have to be a part of it to know. We had an understanding, a way of communicating, and even a method of dealing with personal struggles that inevitably came up. A group of people sharing a common experience.

I will never forget that painful year of cancer treatment. It changed my life and made me who I am. You learn to look at your life differently when you almost lose it.

In the same way, I will never forget my experience with Team In Training. I was able to heal, grow and make a difference all at the same time.

When life comes full circle, it is encouraging to know you can be triumphant with the help of relationships, determination that is unbreakable, and strength that only grows stronger over time.

Team In Training Spotlight:
"Cancer Brought Me Closer to God"
– Judy Gillette, a survivor's story

Judy Gillette is a patient who has Waldenstrom's macroglobulinemia (also known as lympho-plasmacytic lymphoma or immunocytoma), a rare, slow-growing B-cell lymphoma that occurs in less than 2 percent of people with non-Hodgkin's lymphoma. Judy has been battling her cancer on and off for almost a decade. Her son, Brian Gillette, sits on the board of the Leukemia & Lymphoma Society's Des Moines chapter.
In her own words.

I taught Sunday school all my life and went to church, but I had no idea what a close relationship with God could be until I was diagnosed with cancer. I really reached out for Him.

Before, I'd never thought so much about praying for myself – I prayed for other people. But, it was like the Holy Spirit came upon me and said, "You do pray for yourself. I am listening. I am here." It was a real experience for me.

And this sounds so hokey, but there have been times, like on my way to treatments when I was nervous and tense, that some message would come across the radio that I knew was intended for me to hear – and it was really, really incredible. One of them was, "Why are you worrying? God is with you. He is always with you." It made me smile like, "Yeah, why am I worrying because He is there; He is with me and He knows."

When you have cancer, you are totally out of control. You no longer have any control of your life and, at some point, I realized that I had to turn my life over to God. He would know the answers and lead me in the right direction – even, maybe, the way He's led me to you. I thought about that because I hope I can do or say something that means something for some other person in their journey. So, I even think that you and I are talking because of that.

I don't know if you know it or not, but I am a tennis player. I have actually been to sectionals and the USTA nationals. The first time I had treatment, I thought, "Oh, I've got to quit playing tennis" because I didn't think I could complete treatments and continue playing tennis. But, I found out that I could. All the treatments since then, I've continued with all my leagues. I also walk three miles most days. I lift weights and do stretching exercises. Even at 69, I'm an athlete.

I don't think I would still be here if it wasn't for rituximab (Rituxan), just flat out wouldn't be here. Rituxan was directly related to the fundraising from Team In Training. My son Brian, who's on the board of LLS, told me that. Rituxan has given me a way to remain active in society. In fact, when I die, I don't want anybody to say "Poor Judy, she suffered so long." I'm not saying I didn't go through tough times and even relapse, but I always kind of knew in the back of my mind that, in a few days or a week or two, I'd be back on track. I always kind of looked at those relapses as being human.

I've enjoyed the last eight years. I've made sure I'm doing a little more in the church. I'm teaching Sunday school. I'm on the outreach committee, and I have worked on backpacks for school, a prison ministry and Habitat for Humanity.

I believe God uses people, like He uses you to put this in writing. Everything goes back to how God uses people to perform what he wants to happen. He's put quite a few people in front of me who've had cancer, who are going through chemotherapy. I know what my emotional needs were at that point; I know God put these people in front of me so I could give them encouragement to never give up.

I remember, it would have probably been November of 2010, I was really sick. I became septic, and I ended up in the hospital for nine days. The church had made a prayer shawl, praying over it the whole time they were making it. And that was one of those experiences, you know, when the minister laid that shawl over me, the warmth just radiated through me.

How many people have you run into that have said cancer was a blessing because it brought them closer to God? I heard that in the beginning, and I thought, "How can that be true?" But you know what, that's the way I feel.

The Battle against Cancer:
On the Front Lines

Meet cancer fighter Kristin Greiss, Nurse, Oncology Case manager, RN, BSN, OCN

When Kristin was in nursing school, she said there were two areas she didn't want to go into: cancer and burns. That's until she was thrown into an internship on the cancer floor – and loved it. "I loved the people, and this sounds ridiculous, but I loved going through something really hard with people, being able to help make that a little less awful. I've been in oncology ever since."

When you have a patient coming in to hear their diagnosis for the first time, what goes through your mind? How do you prepare?
It's hard to prepare because you know that somebody's life is going to be changed forever after they come in. Usually, they know a diagnosis is coming. They know they have a lymphoma or a type of something, but they don't know what that means – they just know it's cancer. They are obviously scared, and I think it's my role to be there, to be supportive and to help them any way I can.

What do I do to prepare? This is me personally – I have a strong Christian faith, and I draw from that a lot because I don't think I could do this if I didn't. I think it would be too difficult.

And hope. I just think I have hope that people are going to do well. Dr. Armitage deals with lymphoma patients, and with lymphoma, in general, the prognoses are pretty good. I think that's why I'm hopeful too because no matter where somebody is right now, there's hope that six months from now or a year from now, they're going to be okay. That's not always the case, but there's hope. I think to give people hope is important.

What happened on the toughest day of your job?
There are a lot of hard days. You can get really attached to patients, and they become friends. So, it's more than medicine; it's dealing with someone that you have a relationship with.

I was very attached to one patient who had five children, the oldest was a senior in high school. She had been through all of her treatments and had a bone marrow transplant – and then she came down with a weird infection. It was actually kind of unheard of.

As we were figuring out what it was, Dr. Armitage and I were scheduled to go to a meeting in Hawaii. So, the timing was very sad because here's this person I care about who's sick and in the hospital with this weird – and incurable – infection. We had to leave for this meeting knowing that it was not going to turn out well. It was a really awful feeling. I was in Hawaii and I got word that she had passed away. Her kids had just lost their mother; her husband had lost his wife. That was one of the worst days.

Let's switch and talk about your best days.
The best days are, obviously, when things go well and people get good news, when they hear: "Your cancer's gone!" or "You're in remission!" That's a priceless experience. When people hear, "We can't find your cancer. Everything you've been through, it's worked; it's paid off." That's the best day.

I remember this young gal, she was probably 25, who had a diagnosis of Hodgkin lymphoma. She was looking forward to starting her life and her job, and now had this diagnosis of cancer.

She was very outgoing and very ambitious, and she wanted to be treated very fast to get on top of it. So, she came in with her boyfriend for her bone marrow biopsy and her PET scan, and I went over to meet her for the first time in the treatment center.

For a time there, I was alone with her boyfriend, and I said, "This has to be really scary for you too because it's not only affecting her, it's affecting your future and your life."

He said, "It made me realize that I don't want another day in my life without this girl."

So, he's getting emotional, and I'm getting emotional. Then, he said, "I haven't told anybody this, but I went out and bought a ring. I'm going to propose to her this weekend."

Now, I'm sobbing like a baby. When she comes back into the room, we're both sitting there crying, and she thinks we're talking about her prognosis. I can't ruin his secret so I just say, "We were talking about how scary this is, that we're going to fight it, and that he is here with you. You're lucky. He's a good guy."

Now, 2 and ½ years later, she's gone through all of her treatments, and they just had their first baby. It feels like they are family almost. There are a lot of good stories like that.

°Do you know any patients who have been involved in Team In Training or who've had family members participate?
There's a patient whose daughter has done somewhere between 15-20 events for Team In Training.

It's an uplifting motivator for patients when somebody cares. It's very special for patients to know that someone would sacrifice and put their time and energy into something that will make a difference in their lives or other people's lives. It seems a lot of patients are very selfless and know that, even if it doesn't help them, it's going to help hundreds if not thousands of other people.

Team In Training is the fundraising arm for research for the Leukemia & Lymphoma Society. What is your impression of the advances that are being made?
Here at the University of Nebraska Medical Center, we are very involved with research. There are patients who are alive today because of things that have come out in the eleven years that I've been here that wouldn't have been otherwise. So for sure, they are making huge advances in the research and treatments.

Here's an example: There was a patient with myeloma who was probably within days to weeks of the end of his life. But, he got onto a recent trial and is now doing great, working and enjoying life. It's exciting. Knowing that the research is being done really does give people the hope to hang on or to keep going.

Rituximab (Rituxan), which is a lymphoma drug, was approved in 1997. It's made a huge, huge difference, probably one of the biggest differences in the cancer world, for outcomes for lymphoma patients.

What do you think is the most important lesson you've learned from your patients?
I get to experience this difficult journey with people, and I think I've learned to love people more and value less the things that don't really matter in my life.

Seven

FUNDRAISING 101: THE MONEY & THE MISSION

"Whether donating blood, stem cells, money or volunteering your time, these little things make such a big difference in people's lives. This is the definition of TEAM – 'ordinary' people doing extraordinary things." – **Jenna Hardy, TNT athlete**

"Have you heard enough about Team In Training for one flight, Richard?" I asked. "Are you dying to peruse that in-flight magazine?"

"Not at all," he said. "I find it all very interesting."

"You're getting the full rundown today – an oratorical marathon," I replied.

"This army of Team In Training athletes, they didn't know my family; they didn't know Cheryl, but they impacted us, and I really appreciate that," he said. "This group, this Team is making a real difference in a lot of lives – and that's something to be proud of."

"You know, as coaches, our role is to help train our athletes so they can accomplish these insane physical challenges. But, at its heart, Team In Training wasn't designed to be a training program with a fundraising component; it was designed to be a fundraising program – with a training component."

"How much money have all of those athletes raise again?" Richard asked.

"More than 600,000 athletes – about 1.4 billion dollars."

"Billion with a 'b'?" he clarified.

"Billion with a 'b,'" I answered. "And no less than 75 percent of every dollar donated to LLS directly supports the Society's mission."

"Amazing," he said. "And what… you all hold fundraisers? Get sponsors? How does that work?"

"Every athlete has to raise a certain amount of money. It varies event-to-event, whatever is needed to ensure that 75 percent going back to the mission after athlete expenses are paid: lodging, race registration, administrative support. Fundraising strategies vary, from letter writing campaigns to golf tournaments and Oscar-watching parties. We had a couple of athletes who'd invite everyone over for this massive pulled pork feast – 'Pork-a-Polooza' they called it."

I continued, "Kelly and I funded our first several Team In Training events with letters. I still remember sitting down at the computer, typing with tears streaming down our faces – the catharsis of it all…"

Dear Family and Friends,

This is not an ordinary letter. It is, perhaps, one of the most important we will ever compose. We are writing to humbly ask for your support and your prayers.

Bob Seger summed it up so gracefully in his ode to perseverance, Against the Wind -- "I wish I didn't know now what I didn't know then."

Not so long ago, we didn't know the special heartache involved in witnessing a loved one wrestle with cancer. We know it now – and we know that we are compelled to act.

On June 6th, Kelly will participate in the <u>Leukemia & Lymphoma Society's</u> "Rock and Roll Marathon" in honor of Sharon Bearden and the millions like her who are living in the shadow of this despicable disease.

It is our goal to raise $3,500 for the Society and its fight against leukemia and other blood based cancers. So, with hat in hand, we are calling on you for your sponsorship and pleading for your generosity.

The cause could not be worthier. Almost everyone touched by cancer has also been witness to the Society's important work. It was instrumental in developing the treatments we rely on today: chemotherapy, radiation, and bone marrow transplantation. Since 1960, the survival rate for the most common form of childhood leukemia has jumped from 4% to more than 90%.

Every dollar you donate brings us one step closer to our goal, but, more importantly, it brings us closer to the goal we all share – a cure for cancer. Be assured, at least 75% of your contribution will directly support the research and development of treatments.

We know now that we are all in this together. We have heard too many stories to suggest otherwise – too many stories about husbands who've lost wives, daughters who've lost mothers and fathers who've lost sons.

We know now what the face of bravery looks like. We see it every time we flip open the family album.

We know now that we can fight or we can run. God willing, for our part, we chose to do both.

Thank you in advance for your prayers and support.

Survival Rates Rising

"The Leukemia & Lymphoma Society funds research across the continuum, from basic research through clinical trials, from bench to bedside. To date, we have invested almost $1 billion in research to advance therapies and save lives. LLS research grants have funded many of today's most promising advances, including targeted therapies and immunotherapies and some of the therapies first approved for blood cancer patients are now helping patients with other types of cancers and other serious diseases. Thanks to research and access to better treatments, survival rates for many blood cancer patients have doubled, tripled and even quadrupled since 1960."[8]

---

[8] www.lls.org

Athlete Reflections:
A Giver Who Kept on Giving
- Jenna Hardy, TNT athlete

Jenna gets goose bumps every time she shares this story. Her father, David Hardy, was diagnosed with chronic lymphocytic leukemia (CLL) at the age of 40. He passed away at the age of 52, one and a half years after receiving a stem cell transplant.

"His journey is a remarkable story within itself, but this isn't just about him" Jenna said. "This is about a stranger who made an extraordinary impact on my father, our family, and especially me."

For 10 years, occasional chemotherapy held David's cancer at bay, but the day came when his oncologist informed him the disease was getting worse and chemotherapy was no longer effective. It was time for a stem cell transplant. Since his siblings were not bone marrow matches, an unrelated donor needed to be identified.

Around this same time, a 27-year-old man in Texas placed his name on the bone marrow donor registry. A short two months later, Justin received the call. He was a match for Jenna's father. Would he agree to donate his stem cells?

"My father received Justin's stem cells on January 10, 2007, considered his 'new birthday.' The stem cells did their job and rid his body of leukemia, but my father developed a side effect, common when receiving stem cells from an unrelated donor, called Graft vs. Host Disease. This is a form of rejection, in which the donor's cells attack the recipient's organs. It attacked my father's skin, liver and eventually his intestinal tract," Jenna said.

If the two parties agree, a donor and recipient are allowed to meet one year after a transplant. Justin immediately requested to meet David, and David felt the same about wanting to meet Justin.

"We were able to fly Justin and his wife to California for the City of Hope Annual Transplant Survivor's Celebration. We, also, had a party at our house to thank Justin for his gift of life. My father, who had been struggling terribly, was stronger during Justin's visit," Jenna said.

Her father passed away on June 25, 2008, after a long battle with Graft vs. Host Disease.

"Two years later, I found myself out of college and in San Diego, California. I was on my way to my first day of my 'big girl' job when I heard an ad on the radio about Team In Training: 'Come on out, join Team and help fight blood cancers.'

"Dad, is that you? If this wasn't a calling for me, I don't know what would be! I immediately signed up and was training with the Team that Saturday. That night, I set up my fundraising page so I could start asking for donations," she recalled.

She needed to raise was $2,000 and posted an appeal on Facebook, thinking she would get a couple donations from friends. That following Tuesday, her mom called: "How the heck did you already reach your minimum?!"

What was she talking about? It was impossible to be at $2,000 already, Jenna thought.

"But, I checked my Team In Training fundraising page, and it read, '$2,000. 100% minimum reached.'"

Jenna checked the donor list, and there it was – a $2000 donation. From Justin.

"The man who donated his stem cells, gave my father another shot at life and gave my family another year to be with him also gave me $2,000 to reach my goal and fund life-saving research," said Jenna.

She continued, "My family can't thank Justin enough for all he has done for us. I hope this story shows you how people can really make a difference. Whether donating blood, stem cells, money or volunteering your time, these little things make such a big difference in people's lives. This is the definition of TEAM – 'ordinary' people doing extraordinary things. Like our 'ordinary' friend from Texas, Justin, our hero."

Someday Is Today.

*T*hanks to your generous support of The Leukemia & Lymphoma Society, this is a new world. Hundreds of thousands of people diagnosed with blood cancer are today living normal, productive lives.

We are on the threshold of amazing breakthroughs. Your money accelerates miraculous new treatments and healing therapies once thought impossible. And with our co-pay and insurance assistance, many patients can now afford the medications they need.

Cures today. Not someday. That's the goal. And you are at the heart of it. [9]

Athlete's Journey:
Katie Sullivan Poppert's Story – Part III

*K*atie figured the fundraising was going to be a really big challenge so she wanted to get started on that right away.

"Did I mention that I graduated from college in three years instead of four and nursing school in one year instead of two? Yes, I admit it – I'm a bit of an overachiever," she said. "So if they said I needed to raise $4200, I was going to raise $5000 or $6000... Dare I say $10,000?"

The only problem – she had never done any fundraising on her own before so she had no real idea how difficult it could be, or just how many people, hours, and, yes, blood, sweat and tears it would take.

"As I was preparing my body for the torture of the race, I was constantly aware of the fundraising that I needed to do and just how important that money really was. I would hit up everyone I knew. I would call upon the talents and energy of my friends and family with no guilt. I would host my first fundraising party," she said.

Like most people, Katie had attended her fair share of these parties – but she had no idea just how much work went on behind the scenes. She wanted to be sure people had a good time while opening up their wallets.

---

[9] www.lls.org

She needed a band. She needed food. She needed booze. She needed items for the auction.

"And I needed an appointment with a shrink to figure out why I thought I was capable of all of this, in addition to training, kids, and work," Katie said.

She continued, "I am lucky enough to be raising my kids in the same swim and tennis club that I spent my childhood summers in. Since you can rent it out for parties, I figured this would be a good venue for the fundraiser. What I didn't figure on, however, was just how much stress was involved in the praying/dancing/bargaining for good weather so I could actually host this thing at an outdoor venue. I was becoming addicted to weather.com and would check several times a day, just to see if anything had changed."

The party was set for a Saturday in late August. Monday came. It rained. Tuesday came. It rained again. Wednesday came. It rained AND hailed a bit. Thursday came. More rain. That Friday, as she was madly scurrying around to gather up last minute items for the party, she was driving in... the rain.

Saturday morning hit. As she peeked precariously outside, Katie was greeted by a brilliant sun and gorgeous blue skies.

As "go time" approached, Katie and Christy sent up one last plea to the weather gods, gave each other a good luck squeeze and turned to face the first guests.

"My husband Todd's sister, Cori, had made a poster board tribute to their brother, Jeff, who died from ALL at the age of eleven and a half. There were pictures of him throughout his short life, many with the tell-tale bald head from the chemotherapy. It was very tough for me to look at, as I see him in each of my children. Also, Liam, my oldest, is about the same age Jeff was when he lost his battle. I can honestly say that I cannot imagine losing him. Period. It makes it difficult to even breathe at the mere thought. I have so much respect and awe for my in-laws, as well as the millions of other parents in the world who have had to do the unthinkable – bury their own children," Katie said.

People stopped to admire the collage of Jeff on their way into the party. Katie's aunts pitched in and organized the silent auction. The

'Bunco girls' and other family members brought food and wine. The band played, people ate and drank.

It turned into a beautiful evening, despite the threat of a band of ominous clouds over the mountains, and Katie could swear she caught a glimpse of Jeff glimmering in the nearby trees, smiling.

"With the success-and stress-of the party behind me, it was time to really focus on my training..."

Team In Training Spotlight:
A Fundraising Phenomenon!
– The Team WillyK Story: Part I

"Team WillyK" is a true Team In Training Phenomenon. Based out of Des Moines, Iowa, Team WillyK is centered on the life of Will Krueger, a now nine-year-old boy whose three-and-a-half year battle with acute lymphoblastic leukemia (ALL) began when he was 4.

To date, Team WillyK has raised over $1,000,000, a mark it eclipsed on June 2, 2013 by bringing 100 fundraising athletes to the San Diego Rock 'n' Roll Marathon, Team WillyK's eighth Team In Training event.

Team WillyK demonstrates the dedication, charity and compassion that is uniquely Team In Training. Their training and fundraising efforts provide a clear representation of the true power (dunamis) of Team In Training – the power and resources arising from numbers and the power consisting or resting in armies, forces or angels.

Nick Krueger, father of Will Krueger and one of five brothers, in his own words

I can't even tell you how long ago, probably 12 years ago, my wife was working for a gentleman who did a ton of stuff for LLS. At the time, he was doing a marathon a day for six or seven days across the Sahara desert, and he was doing all of it in honor of a little girl who had ALL (acute lymphoblastic leukemia).

He actually had someone donate a Harley Davidson for a raffle, and he was selling 200 tickets at $100 each. We bought a ticket – and wound up winning this thing.

My wife always kept the raffle ticket in her wallet as a reminder of how lucky we were. Our goal was to give the value back, over time, to LLS.

Now fast forward to 2007. My father-in-law was diagnosed with CLL (chronic lymphocytic leukemia) and passed away that September. Then our son was diagnosed in February of 2008.

The Diagnosis: Acute Lymphoblastic Leukemia

My wife had taken our two boys to Florida to visit her mom, and Will was really sick the whole time he was there. In hindsight, he had all the typical symptoms of leukemia: the white skin, his bones and legs hurt. Even when he was out in the sun, he looked ghostly white. His energy level was terrible. At night, he would sweat profusely.

The night before he was diagnosed, he was up crying in the middle of the night, and his shoulder hurt. I just remember my wife coming back to bed and saying, "I think it is really serious. I think he has cancer."

I was really upset, pissed even: "How dare you say that?" "It's our kid. Don't think that way." All that kind of stuff.

At the doctor's office the next day, I could see the doctors talking, and I knew something was really wrong. I could see it on their faces. I was just so grateful that my wife didn't have to get that news without me. Your life changes in an instant; it's just brutal. You never, never forget that moment.

"...Where He Almost Died."

Will wound up having a really long stay in the hospital; he was really sick. There were probably four or five occasions where he almost died.

Probably a week after his initial stay in the hospital, he just wasn't breathing right. I don't know if you've ever been around someone before they pass away, but they do this thing with their lips as they're breathing, their lips almost flutter as they breathe. That's what he was doing. It turned out he had fluid on his heart and lungs, which had to be removed. Probably an hour after the surgery, Will was running around the floor. It was unbelievable, the most incredible thing.

He had all sorts of scares, one thing after another, including an allergic reaction to a bad lot of chemo, but he rallied; he got through it.

Going through It

Going through it, you are just reacting, just trying to be there.

It was tough on Will; he was terrified. Every time his port was accessed, it would take three people to hold him down. His treatment was three years and five months, and it was so emotionally draining seeing him look so defeated.

He had a terrible experience with spinal taps early on. My wife and I physically had to leave the floor because he was screaming so hard. It was the worst experience of my life, worse than you could imagine. Brutal.

I remember, once, having to hold him down during a spinal tap. As a parent, it's not a situation that we wanted to be in nor should we have been in. I just remember him looking at me like "What are you doing to me?!" It just beats you up; it's tough stuff.

I asked him afterwards, "Do you remember Dad holding onto you when you had your spinal tap?" And he said, "Nope." I was like, "I'm never going to do that again."

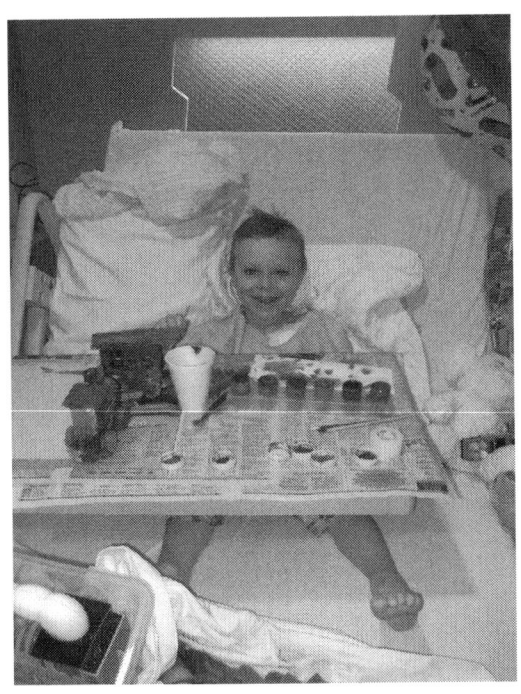

Enter Team In Training

We realized quickly that we didn't have any control over what was going to happen to Will – and that Will would not be alive today if it wasn't for all the research and the people who had gone before him.

So, we figured the least we could do was to raise money. We got to the point where the only thing we could control was raising awareness and raising money for Team In Training.

Scott Krueger, Nick's brother, uncle of Willy K and board member for LLS's Des Moines Chapter, in his own words

I'm the oldest of five brothers, and we're all hockey players. So, we have fight in us, no issue there – and we started going through the battles.

I remember the first time I went to the hospital. I couldn't believe how many kids were in there. That was just brutal, seeing how many people were going through the same crap that we were going through.

We started looking for something we could do. I had a friend, Joel Drake, who's been on the LLS board for years and has always done races. He'd lean on me for fundraising, and I was half-assed at donating. I had a "Just leave me alone"-kind of mentality. Now, here it is, my nephew gets it.

So, three of my brothers and I decided to do the Hy-Vee triathlon the first year it started in Des Moines. We said we would do it with Team In Training and LLS to support Willy and our brother Nick, and let them know that we were behind them.

We also wanted to give back to all the people who sacrificed because if it wasn't for them, Willy would be dead. We know what the odds used to be, and we know what they are now. We wanted to make a difference.

We sent out fundraising emails to people we knew, and my parents did the same thing. I think in about three weeks, we had about $60,000 in the online account. We were just in awe of how many people reached out. And then this light went off, and I thought, "This came in too easily. I have a job to do here."

We had a ton of money left over after Des Moines, so we decided to do the Team In Training race in Washington DC. We had a blast training as a team. Six of use went up there and did it. Afterward, I thought, "What happens if we just blow this thing up?"

Boom!

Event after event, what became known as Team WillyK continued to grow – 28 participants at the Chicago Triathlon, 48 at the Nations Tri in Washington DC, 62 for the century cycle ride around Lake Tahoe.

What we really liked about it was the team concept of working out together, having a couple of beers after a swim or a bike ride. After four years, we'd raised about $660,000. We just went, "Holy cow! We have a chance to hit a million in five years."

We started this to show Nick and Peg that we love them and we support them. Nick has done all the races except the first one. He says he doesn't know if he could have gotten through it if it wasn't for the Team.

The power of Team is that it is so much stronger than ones and twos and threes. We have always believed that. Team WillyK has definitely proven that.

Melanie Brown, our executive director, says, "Never leave us, please."

And, I say, "If it wasn't for you guys, I wouldn't have my nephew. I am here until I am gone."

Nick Krueger, father of Will Krueger (Cont.)

All of the sudden, we were at $720,000 after, I think, five events as a group. I remember talking to a guy on the LLS Board, and he said, "You know Nick, we've got one shot at a million dollars, just think about it."

I thought, "There's no way. We'd have to recruit over 100 people, and I just don't see us being able to do that." This is where I credit my brother, Scott, and Scott Campney, who we call "Bossman." They said, "We gotta make this million happen."

That changed the dynamics of everything.

Scott Campney, also known as "Bossman" and the "marketing and idea guy," in his own words

Nick Krueger is one of my best friends. I got a phone call one day from Scott (Nick's brother), very emotional, and he was telling me that Will had cancer. That's devastating when you hear that.

Will and my daughter are the same age; they're friends. I remember going to the hospital and feeling like there was nothing I could do. After I heard about Team In Training from Scott, we just said, "We have to do something to make this big."

I had never done any endurance events before; I didn't know if I could. I remember talking to one of the coaches, asking him, "Can you get me to the finish line?" "Oh absolutely, we can get you there," he said, just being nonchalant about it. I left thinking, "Oh my God, I don't know if he is serious or what."

For me, the motivation for that first race was all Will. Every time I'd consider not completing a workout, I'd just think, "Here's this kid going to take these treatments, going through all of this, and I'm only trying to get through a swimming workout!" I used that as motivation almost every workout; it was always on my mind.

I think our first event, each athlete had to raise $4,000 or so, and that can be overwhelming as well. But, if you go out there and actually try to fund raise, if you ask the question, it is amazing how people will help you.

At first, Nick wasn't sure if he wanted to use Will's name. I kind of highly suggested that we needed an identity, and what a cool way for Will to know that there are so many people out there cheering for him.

For that first race (The Hy-Vee Triathlon in Des Moines), I made up shirts. The logo was a railroad track with Thomas the Train on it and a 'W' in the middle.

I remember sitting in the hospital one night. Will, Nick and Peggy, and my daughter, Casey, were all there. Will and Casey were playing with a big circle train track. Will would push the train partway around the circle, and Casey would take it the rest of the way. He said something like, "The circle is so big I can't push the train myself. You're going to have to help me."

To me, it was the perfect quote – and we put it on the back of the shirt.

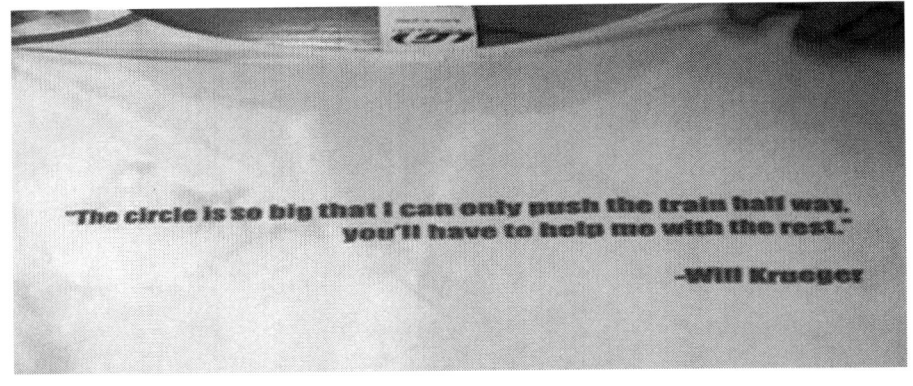

Nick Krueger, father of Will Krueger (Cont.)

Let me tell you about the day Will was done with treatments. So this was June 3, 2011. My brother, Scott, sent a note to all the people on our Team: *"I've seen my kid get an 'A' on an exam. I've seen him hit a home run and score the game-winning run, but can you imagine what it would be like to see your kid beat cancer? That is something that it is amazing! And I think I am going to be there to be a part of it, to help Will celebrate. And our family is going to be there. If you have time to break away and be there, great!"*

After Will's last spinal tap, when we came down the elevator to the main lobby of the hospital, oh man, it was so unbelievable – all the people! My family was there in front. I can't even remember what they were cheering for him, but they had some kind of chant.

The cool thing was – that day was also my younger son's half birthday, so we kind of made it about both boys. I think one of the things, as kids go through this, the siblings can often feel left out. So, it was a neat way for him to think it was, in part, for him too.

The Coolest Day of His Life

The boys came home from the zoo after the treatment, and the house was filled with balloons, the driveway was lined with balloons. Will told us that it was the best day of his life and the coolest day of his life. It was, by far, one of the coolest days of my life too, without a doubt.

Eight

Heart of the Season

"The only thing that got me through the training was thinking about what a cancer patient must go through every day – what their bodies must feel like after each and every chemo or radiation treatment. I thanked God every day that I wasn't vomiting and weak from sickness. This was my fuel source." – **Julie Petersen, TNT athlete**

"From this point on, we are running half marathons or more every Saturday. I thought about that a little and for the first time, got really nervous. Keep us in your prayers." – **Scott J. McCoid, TNT athlete (from his training blog)**

"How long do your training seasons typically last?" Richard asked as we drew ever closer to our shared destination.

"18-to-20 weeks. Sometime a little longer, sometimes a little shorter," I replied. "We trudge through some stuff together during that time: summer heat, winter cold, knee pain, foot pain, waning motivation... All part of the deal. If it was easy, everyone would have marathon medals around their necks, right?"

He nodded and chuckled in agreement. "I suppose so."

I continued, "The heart of the season hits, you're hungry all the time; your body is tired, but at the same time, you know this really cool transformation is taking place. When my athletes start to lose perspective – that is one of my favorite parts of the season. 'Oh,' someone will say, 'I just had the most terrible 8 mile run!' And, I'd have to remind them that five weeks ago, they could barely cover a fourth of that.

"It's our job, as coaches, to keep everyone moving forward. That's what endurance training is all about – keep moving forward. We do our best to motivate, to keep everyone focused on the mission, and we assure everyone that there is, in fact, a finish line waiting for them – and that they will eventually get there. Eventually. Celebrate the good runs; trudge through the bad ones – and know that we are all in this together."

----- **Original Message** -----
From: Coach Dan, Team In Training
Hey Team,

As we push deeper into the season here, I wanted to take a minute to share one of my favorite training stories...

It was a Wednesday night run a while back, and I'll be honest, I was dreading it. It had been a long, hectic day that started way too early. I missed a chance at an afternoon run, which meant pounding the pavement in the dark in my neighborhood while most of my neighbors were catching the tail end of "CSI" or sawing logs. I was tired; I had a headache. While putting the kids to bed, the voices started, "Just skip it... do it tomorrow... you're not up for this..."

As much as I wanted to crawl under the covers, I grudgingly pulled on my purple training shirt and laced up my shoes.

Stepping out the front door into the dark, it hit me immediately – the cool air and the light breeze. This is promising, I thought.

Now, our training can be complicated, so much talk about nutrition and injury prevention and equipment, but that Wednesday night at 9:30 p.m., it was back to the basics for me, focusing on simply putting one foot in front of the other. After a few minutes of creakiness (and to my great surprise), it started to kick in. I felt like I was gliding. Not sure how long the feeling would last, I charged uphill and coasted downhill, the cool air and my iPod keeping me company.

"No, I won't back down..." wailed Tom Petty, right on cue.

As I pushed on, another remarkable thing happened: One of my subdivision neighbors and a longtime TNT honored hero drove by and gave me a wave. It was back to the basics AGAIN for me, a vivid reminder of what this is all about. It's not about me. It's about HER; it's about my sister and mother-in-law and your loved ones and friends – all of those people who have battled or are bravely battling this hideous disease.

I was energized. The purple jersey that I grudgingly pulled on now felt so good on my back. How proud I was and am to be part of TEAM IN TRAINING, part of this Team. How fortunate I am to be able to run for others; coach dedicated, remarkable athletes; and fight cancer in my own way.

I'm certain God has better things to do with His time, but I know He was there for me that Wednesday night, providing a boost, sending signs and strength and cool breezes.

I arrived back home just in time to take a shower and watch my "The Office" re-runs. Added bonus: There was just the right amount of super fudge brownie frozen yogurt left in the container. (Proper rewards are a key part of this whole deal, I cannot stress that enough...)

So, what's the point of this little diatribe. It's a reminder from your coach (if you needed one) that we're all human & we're all in this together. When we have our off-moments, we benefit from getting back to the basics. We lace up our shoes; we push on one step at a time and we focus on the mission. Inevitably, we will be rewarded for our efforts.

Let's face it, what we do isn't always fun. It's a lot of time away from friends and family. It's hard, sweaty, achy work. BUT, while not always fun, it should always be rewarding. There is a finish line, and you will cross it – and you will forever be changed people when you do.

It is impossible to thank you enough your heart and your dedication. Your sacrifice is helping to alleviate the suffering of others. Is there a *higher form of service? You are heroes! You are remarkable! I am privileged to be in your company. Go Team!*

Coach,

Thank you for sharing – your story encourages and refreshes my soul!

Even though God has a lot of important business to attend to, I believe there is nothing more important to Him than taking delight in His children (that's us). I believe it gives Him much pleasure to run with us, especially when our heart's desire is to serve the hurting among us.

Zephaniah 3:17 reads: "The Lord your God in your midst, the mighty one, will save; He will rejoice over you with gladness, He will quiet you with His love, He will rejoice over you with singing!"

Be blessed friends, and while you're running on behalf of those who cannot, know that God is rejoicing over you with every step!

Athlete Reflections:
"It Was a Headache, Not Cancer."
- Shannon Snow, TNT athlete (from her training blog)

Well, I skipped my run yesterday. In my defense, I had a headache. Yep, a headache. Granted, it was a bad one, but it was a headache – not cancer – and I chose to skip my run.

Today, I couldn't escape the guilt, the guilt that I chose not to train because I had a headache. So I made a promise to myself, my friend, Michael, who survived leukemia, and all the sufferers/survivors of blood cancers that I would run my little booty off for them. And I did.

I only had a 3 mile run today, something that I've conquered many times in the past. However, I promised that today I would do it efficiently and alone. Usually when I run solo, it's difficult because I get lazy. But not today. I promised I wouldn't and I didn't.

The first half of the run was painless, I felt great and was making record time. Then I hit the turn-around and the mental exhaustion hit as it almost always does on the back half. I remembered the cancer patients I'm running for. They kept me going.

I remembered my friend, Susan, talking about her mother who suffers from melanoma. Although it's not a blood cancer, the important research the Leukemia & Lymphoma Society does has benefits to all cancers. Susan informed me that her mother wakes up every day knowing this disease will get her, but she just keeps on living and has done so for over a decade. This woman has accomplished so much more than three measly miles – she accomplished life.

As I finished my third mile at a near-record pace for me, I cried. I cried because I can. I can run, I can live, and I can improve the lives of those with blood cancers. I can do this. I will do this. I will do it for them.

Coaches' Inbox:
Heart of the Season

Hey Coach,

Did you know that WIND is a four letter word? At least that is what my husband and I have declared it (placed alongside other four letter words that we're just not supposed to say).

I think it was a combination of hills and wind, but my knee was strongly disagreeing with the whole run thing today.

When people find out that I like to run, I like to point out to them that what I do is more of a glorified shuffle. Yesterday, my last two miles gave all new meaning to the phrase.

Hi Coaches,

Why is it that "non-runners" feel the need to provide you with every horror story about marathon runners possible!? In the last couple of weeks, I have been told how young, healthy people just collapse and die on the course for no reason and how "so-and-so" did a marathon once and would never do it again because it was so painful. I also get the "you should probably just stick with the half-marathon, it will be easier on your body."

Any tips on how to respond, or not respond, to these statements without getting super angry! Grrrr...

Hey there,

Coach here – Let's start with a quote: **"One of the greatest pleasures in life is doing what others say you cannot do."** – Walter Bagehot. Post that on the bathroom mirror and repeat it every morning. It is so true.

You have buzzing about what one of our athletes called "harassment angels" as opposed to guardian angels. He used them for motivation, and I suggest you do the same.

They say, "You shouldn't be doing this. I heard from a friend of a friend that thousands of people drop dead on marathon courses, like, every weekend. I also heard marathon runners poop their pants during the race. For goodness sake... THEY POOP THEIR PANTS."

Though I'm sure there is genuine concern for your well-being (and that of your running wear), in my experience, a lot of people also go negative out of **jealousy** because you're doing something they want to do – but will not do – for themselves. I say "will not" because everyone has the capacity to make healthy changes in their life (whether it's training for a race, eating better or losing weight); they just choose not to. "I don't have the time. I'm too old. I'm too out-of-shape. My kids have soccer... excuse, excuse, excuse..."

Guess what?

We all have burdens. Some of us – like you – say, you know what, I'm doing it anyway. This is something I can do for me and for a great cause – and I'm doing it.

Harassment angels. We all have them. I remember when I was in my own personal funk years ago and needed to drop 35 pounds. I started exercising and eating healthier, and a chubby co-worker snarked, "I'd eat better, but I want to enjoy life..." Oh o.k., because it's so much fun getting winded walking to the mailbox...

Bottom line – Use their negativity/jealousy as fuel and always believe in yourself, what you're doing and why you're doing it.

*How do you respond? Let them know, quite simply, that you are training **the right way:** You're following a proven plan and you have coaches who care deeply about you and are doing their best to minimize risk.*

Explain why you're doing this. It's not about you; it's about something much bigger than all of us. It's about the cause and those who are still fighting. (Then segue gracefully into a reminder of how you're still accepting donations.)

Just be honest. Tell them it's one of the hardest things you've ever done, but it's also going to be one of the most rewarding. And assure them, once and for all, that you will not poop your pants on the course...

Athlete's Journey:
Katie Sullivan Poppert's Story – Part IV

The miles just kept adding up. One foot in front of the other. While Katie was trying desperately to build up her athletic stamina, she was also working on gathering up her mental courage. It was becoming harder and harder to stay motivated, more and more difficult to wake up early, put in the hours. She had gone through one pair of running shoes, had formed huge calluses on both feet – and had yet to break 20 miles.

Then, just when she had about had it, it happened. She wrecked on her scooter, taking a large, crescent-shaped piece of tissue out of her right calf.

"As I sat around feeling sorry for myself it hit me: How many of my patients go into remission, only to relapse later? How many times were they forced to go on after some setback?"

That's all it took. Renewed and recharged, she hit the pavement once again. Those first few miles were always the hardest. Once she hit five or six miles, she went into auto-pilot. Her mind would begin to wander as she became hypnotized by the repetitive motion of her steps. There was even an hour or two that she actually enjoyed herself. Beautiful day, good music, away from the chaos of work and four kids. Just her, the dog, and a clear Colorado sky.

"Although I had many offers from people to join me on my walks, I usually preferred to walk alone, set my own pace – unless Christy was in the mood to slow down for a few miles with me. Those walks seemed to fly by. We never once ran out of things to talk about. There were times when I would just look over at her and tear up. THIS is where my friend should be – outside, laughing and smiling, not in some hospital getting pumped full of chemotherapy or radiation," Katie said.

She continued, "I truly believe that every person needs all kinds of love to complete them. There's just no way for a spouse to be everything to their mate. This is why friendships are so important. Christy just fit into my world so completely that I felt like something was missing if I didn't see her for a few days. Christy, being a church-going Catholic, likes to say that God puts people in your life for a reason. While I am still undecided about the exact presence of God and how He fits into the whole energy/universe thing, the truth of these words seemed to shimmer around us whenever we were together."

Coaches' Inbox:
Heart of the Season

Coach,

You said to tell you if there's a running problem. I hit an impasse this past week that's puzzling. It doesn't have to do with injury but energy. It's possibly linked to stress over my Dad not doing well in the end stages of his CLL, but since I returned home last week, I've had zero energy on every run – like a car with no gas.

Hey Coaches,

I just wanted to send you a quick line... I am in need of some motivation.

I was supposed to run 21-22 miles today, but before I even started running, I was beat mentally. It was 85 degrees; I was tired; I started getting sick last night; and I was running by myself.

At about five miles in, I was a wreck. I had to stop and sit on a hill facing the lake, and I just started weeping for about 15 minutes. It was a mix of not feeling completely motivated to run 21 miles, being physically exhausting and missing my best friend so much.

It's just hard to know that I was able to do 19 last weekend and could only do 7.4 this weekend – and this was supposed to be my peak run. I will try again next week, but until then, I am asking for some motivation.

Coaches,

To be honest, I have been failing at my running schedule since the first 10 miler a few weeks ago. It is a combination of things (shins, exhaustion, blazing heat, life...) and am currently feeling a little defeated. I hope you can help me get back on track. I think my problem is finding that balance and keeping motivated.

----- Original Message -----
From: Your Team In Training Coaches
Team,

We all have our down days when it's hot, we're tired and we just don't want to train... Here's where we have an advantage over you: We know that all of this toil is building to something absolutely amazing. When you cross that finish line, you will regret nothing because you will be something very few people in this world can claim to be – you will be marathoners! And, it will be your accomplishment – you – nobody sweated it out for you on those weekday runs; nobody ran those 26.2 miles for you on race day – all you.

That said, it is normal for motivation to wane at times. So, what do we do about it?

We change our mindset.

Instead of looking at your almost daily training as a chore – as a "to-do" – look at it as a reward.

That training time is YOUR time – no email, no phone calls, no kids pulling on your leg or fighting with their siblings (we love them, but... you know...). It's your time to think (or not think) to listen to music or revel in the silence.

You may never allow yourself this much time – for yourself – ever again. Soak it up. Let it refresh and recharge you. Training time is your reward for venturing beyond your comfort zone, and it's going to culminate in an experience you will NEVER forget.

And, we remind ourselves WHY we're doing this.

As TNT athletes, we have especially powerful motivation. There is an element of personal glory in what we do – no doubt about it – but what really fuels us is the belief that we are running for others, that we are running to save lives. We are running for those who can't. We are running in honor; we are running in memory, we are running to make a difference in the world.

Need something to remind you of that every time you put on your shoes? Pop Melissa Ethridge's "I Run for Life" onto your iPod. "I run for hope. I run to feel. I run for the truth, for all that is real. I run for your mother, your sister, your wife. I run for you & me my friend. I run for life." That is you! You are heroes! Don't ever forget that every step you take is helping stomp out the scourge that is cancer.

Advocating for a Cure

"The Leukemia & Lymphoma Society (LLS) advocates public policy positions that accelerate progress toward cures for leukemia, Hodgkin and non-Hodgkin lymphoma and myeloma, and to improve the quality of life of those with blood cancer, along with their friends and families.

"The LLS Office of Public Policy is charged with pursuing LLS's mission through advocacy aimed at governmental decision-makers. After decisive victories in 2013, LLS will continue to focus on using advocacy to work toward a cure and improve the lives of blood cancer patients in 2014 and beyond."[10]

----- Original Message -----
From: You Team In Training Coaches
Hey Team!

We are closing in on the BIG weekend! You all hit the pinnacle of the training schedule on Saturday – the big 20 miler! The next time you run that far, you'll be in San Fran wearing a purple jersey with a number on it while thousands of people cheer you on!

You all are going to do a fabulous job this weekend and beyond – no doubt about it!

Goals that may have seemed unattainable just a couple of months ago are now within reach, demystified by hard work and steady determination.

You all can do this – and will.

God bless & Go Team!

Athlete Reflections:
"20 Miles Is Different from Everything."
– Meghan Fitzpatrick, TNT athlete (from her training blog)

20 miles. 20 miles is different from everything. I had this foolish idea that because I'd run 17 miles before, 20 miles would be just a little more exhausting. Wrong, wrong, wrong. 20 miles is not something one can visualize ahead of time. It's more tiring, more painful, and more time consuming than the brain can concoct. But it's also more

---

[10] www.lls.org

exciting, more enlivening, and more spectacular. (There is a lot of time to cover various emotions when one is running 20 miles.)

Every so often in our lives, we get to take a minute to say, "Wow, I just did something totally incredible." Yesterday was one of those times for me.

Athlete Reflections:
"A Milestone for Sure"
– Scott J. McCoid, TNT athlete (from his training blog)

This one counts as a milestone for sure: 20 miles today with about 10 other teammates at Lake Zorinsky! The air temperature was about 22 degrees, but the winds brought it down to a "feels like" of about 5 or so.

There were no bands at the lake this morning like there will be on race day – just the running mixes we all put together on our iPods. When we finished, the victory party was a little more reserved than the one we will experience in Phoenix – just the handful of Team in Training colleagues left, braving the elements. But we all had victories today! Every step we took past 17 miles put us all at new personal records.

This one was a hard one, and we made it! Thanks to all my teammates, mentors and especially the coaches for helping us break through levels none had thought possible!

We are going to start tapering down our training now, letting our bodies heal to prepare for that last big number of the season – 26.2! I want to thank everyone for their support and sponsorship thus far. When times of doubt enter my head, I just focus back on all of you, your gifts and all of those we are running for. We are fighting to help them create victories like these every day. Your support means more than you know. Thank you.

\-\-\-\-\- **Original Message** \-\-\-\-\-
From: Your Team In Training Coaches
Hey Team,

We are so proud of you – not just for how you performed today, but for all of the hard work that's gotten you to this point!

Has it sunk in yet what you accomplished? You all knocked it out of the park on Saturday, graduation with class – big miles, big milestones on an absolutely perfect morning! We couldn't be more impressed!

There is something so motivating, so inspiring about watching our athletes go farther than they've ever gone before, battling through aches and bouts of fatigue because quitting simply isn't an option. It's a testament to the human spirit and the heart of this team. We coaches and your mentors are fortunate to witness a full dose of it every Saturday!

The good news (or bad news if you're the sentimental type): We have reached the summit and are now in the downhill portion of our training together – "The Magic Taper!"

From now until race day, we'll be steadily decreasing your mileage, a chance for your bodies to rest and recover in advance of the big day. Take full advantage of it.

Go Team!

Team In Training Spotlight:
A Fundraising Phenomenon!
– The Team WillyK Story: Part II

Des Moines, IA-based Team WillyK, a true Team In Training Phenomenon, has raised over $1,000,000, to date, for the Leukemia & Lymphoma Society. The Team rallied in honor of Will Krueger, a now nine-year-old boy whose three-and-a-half year battle with acute lymphoblastic leukemia (ALL) began when he was 4.

Will finished his treatments in June of 2011, but the work of Team WillyK was not complete...

Scott Krueger, uncle of Willy K, in his own words

And now another guy, Matt Mausser, he jumps in to be president of our LLS Board. Matt raised $120,000 and won LLS Man of the Year – and then his kid gets the junk. Now he's a part of Team Willy K and his son Joe... he's the kid we are gunning for.

Matt Mausser, a LLS Man of the Year, Board member and father of 5 year old Joe, a T-cell leukemia patient who was diagnosed just three days after the birth of his brother Cole, in his own words

I guess the hard part was communicating with my wife. I actually had the doctor call my wife because I really didn't know what to say. She came down with her mother. (Both of our mothers were in town because of the birth of our son.)

It was a pretty ominous two hours there. They sat us in this tiny room, like you see on TV, and they drop that bomb on you – your son has a blood cancer.

Joe was admitted to the ICU, and on Sunday, the next day, they did a spinal tap and a bone marrow biopsy. At midnight that night, he started his chemo treatments.

In the first 30 days, his bone marrow had cleared to zero, and he was technically designated as a "low risk rapid responder." All things being equal, he has done a phenomenal job through this. He is in long term maintenance. He will be done with treatment on December 13, 2014. He's doing really well. He is in pre-K now. His hair is starting to come back.

My wife is kind of opposite of me. At first, she wanted to focus inward and let this wash over her a little bit. I immediately sought out a few folks that I knew whose kids had gone through this. The Tuesday after Joe's diagnosis, I had lunch with Nick Krueger, Will's dad, and we just kind of talked and lamented about our situation and how it's going to be okay.

LLS First Connection makes a difference

I also plugged into LLS almost immediately, and they hooked me up through their First Connection correspondence. They put me in contact with a dad whose son had T-cell leukemia. I had probably an hour and a half phone call with him the first time we spoke.

I just feel like what LLS does – pooling funds from Team In Training, Light the Night and Man and Woman of the Year and funding these researchers – propels research forward much quicker, much more efficiently with exponential returns. I want to be a part of that to the greatest extent possible.

It's clear; it's definable where your dollars go. The impact and the success from LLS is very tangible. When you give $100, play in a golf tournament, or do a Team In Training event, you can be very satisfied knowing that your dollars are going to help families in need; they're helping find cures for these blood cancers so that families don't have to hear those words: "Your son has a blood cancer."

Hooked on Team In Training

My first Team In Training event was the century ride at Lake Tahoe with Team WillyK. It was an awesome, awesome group of people, very passionate, very committed. It really makes the experience that much more meaningful. Then I did another century ride, 122 mile ride in Las Vegas.

So, I've just recently been diagnosed with the Team In Training bug. It is just an amazing experience! When my son got ill, I was maybe 220, and now, I am 204. I'm like, "If my son is going to go through this, I want to live to see my kids have kids."

Nick Krueger, Father of Willy K (Cont.)

Everybody does these events for their own reasons but, man, it changes people's lives – not just the people who have been diagnosed with cancer, but the people in the group who've been pretty remarkable.

So, we've got something going, and I think it is pretty unique. Will it go forever? I really don't know. But man, what an awesome, awesome run!

And, the million dollars thing is something that is real, and we are going to do everything that we can to make it happen.

The Battle against Cancer: On the Front Lines

Meet cancer fighter Maribeth Hohenstein, RN, BSN, OCN, a research coordinator with the Lymphoma Program at the University of Nebraska Medical Center. She has worked with the program for more than 18 years.

Why did you choose to work in oncology? What makes a good day for you?
I love the people I work with, the patients and their families. I think they look to us to get strength, but it's really a two-way street. We get so much from our patients. They are so strong, and I really enjoy that. I've seen them go through their struggles, good times and the bad times.

I want to be in a place where I know I can make a difference, and even though it may not always be big things, I feel like I can make a difference for someone. That's really important to me.

In your years of nursing, where have you seen patients draw their strength from to fight their cancer battle?
They dig deep, and a lot of patients have a strong faith. If it is not strong at the time, I think it becomes stronger.

Family is also huge. You can just tell when the family is involved and supportive. I think the patients gain a lot of strength from that extra support from families and friends.

What gains have you seen in the treatments in lymphoma?
One of the top things, over the course of my being here, is the approval of the drug rituximab (Rituxan). That's become part of the standard of care for patients with lymphoma, and it has made significant improvements in outcomes for patients. About 80% of b-cell lymphomas have a protein or antigen on them called a CD-20 antigen, and rituximab actually targets that antigen and induces the immune response so it encourages the patient's own immune system to fight the lymphoma.

Another thing that is happening with research and treatment is that a good number of our newer medications are oral as opposed to intravenous, and, in general, they seem to be better tolerated.

What is some advice that you have for people battling lymphoma?
Stay positive. A good positive attitude will go a long way. That doesn't mean that you're not going to have bad days and sad days, and that's okay. But just keep a good positive attitude. It just makes a huge difference.

Is there one case where a patient really turned it around when you weren't expecting it?
One case that comes to mind: I, recently, enrolled a patient in my study who failed to respond to previous treatments. We were able to get him into remission and get him onto transplant. That's one of those "Wow moments."

Those are the things that everyone needs to hear – that what we're doing is positive and we are making headway. We can't guarantee patients are going to respond. We can't guarantee anything because it is a study. So, to actually have patients respond and do well after they've failed everything else, that's exciting.

What about advice to someone considering a career in oncology, whether it's nursing or research?
I love it. I love the patients, the physicians and the team I work with. Everybody cares. They take the time that the patient needs. We're not in a rush to move on. It's just is a warm, caring environment.

Nine

Heartbreak & Hope

"Eleven hours after lymphoma killed my father, I laced up my shoes and went running. You might think that I am proud of this. I'm not. I'm not embarrassed, either. But it does seem like a callous, self-indulgent reaction, as if I had told my mother, my brothers, and my kids to just marinate in their grief while I got in my exercise. So why'd I do it?" – **A.P. Beemer, TNT athlete**

Part I: Heartbreak

The pilot chimed in over the loudspeaker: "Thanks again for flying with us this afternoon, ladies and gentlemen. We're about 100 miles from San Diego, just beginning our descent now. We should be on the ground in about half-an-hour. Sit back and enjoy the rest of the flight."

"So, how long do you and your wife plan to continue coaching?" Richard asked.

"The day we stop treating it as an absolute privilege is the day we hang up our jerseys," I answered. "Other than that, I think we're in it until our bodies give out – or they cure cancer and let us go."

"That would be a good day," he said.

"The best," I replied.

"What would you say is the hardest part?" he followed.

I paused for a moment to collect my thoughts. "The hardest part is also one of the most rewarding," I said. "Most of what we do as TNT coaches is exactly what you would expect: We set our athletes up with a solid training schedule; we talk about – and troubleshoot issues related to – nutrition, equipment and injury prevention; we cheerlead; we motivate; and we reassure."

I continued, "Counsel. Motivate. Reassure. Day after day. Week after week. The nuts-n-bolts. But, when you're a TNT coach, it can go well beyond that, venturing into a delicate place where 'Stretch after your workout' and 'Eat your carbs,' simply doesn't cut it. That's because an overwhelming majority of our athletes didn't join the Team to simply compete or complete – they come here to heal. They've lost mothers, fathers, brothers, sisters and friends – or they are witnessing a battle unfold. They feel helpless, and they need an antidote to that poison. Along comes that well-timed TNT ad on the radio or a flyer placed in a favorite restaurant. It promises a way to turn their pain into empowerment, a way to make a broad difference. It promises a measure of healing."

I paused for another moment. "TNT staff, mentors and coaches, we're not therapists – just human beings with hearts and the natural empathy that comes from our own experiences of suffering."

Coaches' Inbox:
Heartbreak

Coaches,

It is with a very sad heart to tell you that my father has failed all leukemia treatments and, last week, was put in hospice. He is now dying and on morphine.

It won't be long. I doubt he'll make a day or two. I was hoping to do the Lincoln Half Marathon in honor of him, but it will also be in memory of him.

Coach here – Truly a heartbreaking update… I, too, started my first season "in honor" and finished it "in memory." It is heinous what cancer does to families.

Just like Lance Armstrong saying "It's not about the bike," it's not really about the race anymore… That Sunday in May is going to be a celebration of your father, of all the people who've supported you on this journey, and of the difference you've made with your tremendous efforts.

For now, know that you, your father and your family continue to be in our thoughts and prayers. May God bless you and bring you all comfort.

Hey guys,

I am having some issues with the emotional aspect of everything… I'm the one whose mom was fighting Leukemia. She passed away last week.

My friend is doing a good job at trying to keep me motivated to train, but it's still really difficult! I tell myself this is why I'm doing this, but when it's time for me to hit the road, I just never do, or wind up backing out at the last minute.

Do you have any suggestions? I don't want to get behind in training, but I'm having such a hard time. Help!

Coach here – Our deepest sympathies, our thoughts and our prayers…

Right now, the most important thing for you to be doing is whatever you feel you need to be doing. If running just doesn't fit into the equation at this moment, that's fine. Focus on getting through the day – and focus on letting yourself grieve without putting additional burden on yourself. When the time is right, we'll get you caught up – no worries – we have a long way 'til race day. And if you decide this just isn't the right time for marathon training, that's fine too.

That said, I will also say this, the Team In Training experience, for many of us, is about healing above all. I don't know what you're going through, I only know what I've been through – and, for me, training wasn't something I did in addition to my mourning; it was something I did in conjunction with my mourning. I remember after my sister passed away, running on the Keystone trail, spending time with her in thought, tears streaming down my face. Healing.

The same thing after Kelly's mom passed away – training for a triathlon, biking in a downpour, remembering, having a solid weep and just feeling very close to her (while somehow managing to maintain my balance...). That's actually what it's all about -- maintaining our balance when devastating loss has swept our legs from under us. Training can be that balance provider.

If this is something you want to do – for your mother, for yourself, for the too many whom we'll never meet – then don't give up. You've suffered a seismic loss, but cancer doesn't have to take this experience from you as well. Regain your balance with us; move forward with us – and if you need one of us to show up on your doorstep for a mid-week run, we will be there – and we will be here for you all season long and beyond.

Pray on it. Know that our hearts are broken for your loss – and if you just want to walk & talk about this some evening, we'd be more than happy to meet up.

May God bless you and bring you peace.

Coaches,

I'm sorry it took this long to let you all know, but my dad had a sudden deterioration in his condition last weekend and died Tuesday night in Chicago. I've been in Chicago since last Monday, out of touch for the most part, busy with a whole lot of official stuff related to dad's death. My mom and the rest of the family are making out okay. I'm doing okay, too. My dad is the biggest reason I'm doing TNT and that hasn't changed.

Thanks for all your support.

A.P.

Athlete Reflections:
"Go Running. That's Your Job."
– A.P. Beemer, TNT athlete,
in his own words

March 15, 2011
  1 p.m.

A gated Insta-village in the far western suburbs of Chicago

Eleven hours after lymphoma killed my father, I laced up my shoes and went running. You might think that I am proud of this; I'm not. I'm not embarrassed, either. But it does seem like a callous, self-indulgent reaction – as if I had told my mother, my brothers, and my kids to just marinate in their grief while I got in my exercise. So why'd I do it?

Well, the TNT training schedule said to run eight miles. Dad was big on schedules. If the family road trip was supposed to start at eight in the morning, the Malibu Classic station wagon would pull out of the garage at 8:00, not 7:59, not 8:01. In these matters I do not jest. I was trained well. The schedule said eight miles, so I headed out the door and turned left up a slight rise on dishonestly-named Tuscan View Drive. When at all possible start a grieving run uphill; it encourages cursing.

So the first reason, while honest, is a little thin. Really, why go running? Six weeks before a marathon, one eight mile run is an event that can be rescheduled. The thing is, I didn't want to reschedule. I had been thinking about running all morning, from the groggy awakening after a late, bad night at the hospital, to the surreal encounter with "funeral man" to arrange for Dad's cremation, I wanted, frankly, to run the hell away. I wanted to run all the confused and sad feelings out of me. I hadn't the faintest notion that it wasn't possible, that this new thing was a thing that would linger.

I loped, cursing, up the little hill and turned left to an asphalt path through a wetland area. Cattails, ducks, and muskrats. A big reedy pond. Look for otters in the creek. If you're lucky you can flush a couple deer out of the field of grass or out from a stand of trees. Watch out for cave-ins in the asphalt; muskrat tunnels undermine the path. Turning an ankle on "muskrat path" is no way for your TNT experience to end. And we'd seen enough hospitals that week.

Now I was warmed up. Running in the groove, ten minutes on, one minute of walking, ten minutes on again. At training pace, it would be about an hour and a quarter. The initial thrill of being loose on the earth, out in the fresh air and moving fast. Well, fast enough. I relaxed and settled into the run, and, of course, that's about when I started crying. Ah, Dad...

What in hell was I doing running? I wanted to curl up in a ball, but I kept going, around the pond, along the back path through more fields, onto sidewalks through the residential part of the community. Tears rolling down my face, my eyes hot, my lips a little trembly, I just kept on. Oh, come on, Andy. Go home. Why keep it up?

The bulldog made me do it. My mother, the new widow, the bulldog, tough as only a kid from a family of sixteen can be, she told me to go running. When the widow tells you to do something, you get up and do it. All I did was mention running and she said, quickly and directly, "Go running. That's your job."

It *was* my job. But I think she meant that my running had just gotten a whole lot more serious. It had become everyone's business. What had been a simple commitment to make something decent out of my dad's illness and raise his spirits had now become something else, and that something was no longer just mine. What I had signed up for had changed on me without my consent. I did not want to run as a tribute to my dad, but that's what happened and that was my new job. Don't muck it up, kid.

So I kept running, tears and all, south through the development, along the edges of another pond, across the street to another pond, another field, another muskrat path. I took the path as far south as I could and turned it around towards home, fighting a cold north wind. I ran it back to a couple hundred yards from the house then walked it slowly in, my head aching from crying, my nose the only thing still running. But I did it.

I managed to get my eight miles in without my mind, which was simply scattered, or my heart, which was really too heavy to carry around. That's the true story of my entire last six weeks of TNT. Only part of me was around. My heart and my mind were out looking for my dad, but I still had my legs. They just kept moving, one stride at a time. And sometimes your legs, and maybe a bulldog behind you, are all that you need.

The Battle against Cancer:
On the Front Lines

Dr. Tim Dunnigan, clinical psychologist, on the three possible outcomes of a cancer diagnosis: remission, relapse, death

Most patients and loved ones hope for and believe the patient will recover. Treatments, no matter how 4debilitating, nurture these hopes. Physicians and nurses encourage patient and family. A remission restores faith in one's life. Relapses and deaths betray that hope and faith.

However, all these experiences reveal a common distortion of our lives as humans – our tendency to deny the reality of death. We may know of it and intellectually acknowledge it, but we don't really believe we or those we love will die – not soon anyway.

A number of psychologists believe this "denial of death" is fundamental to many emotional disorders. It is my belief that when patients say they've never felt more alive than when they survived a brush with death or learned of and accepted that they have a potentially terminal illness, it is because they really accept that death can always be just around the corner.

The theme of "memento mori" is old in the arts and culture. According to Wikipedia, "As a Roman general was parading through the streets during a victory triumph, standing behind him was his slave, tasked with reminding the general that, although at his peak today, tomorrow he could fall, or more likely, be brought down. The servant is thought to have conveyed this with the warning, 'Memento mori.'"

We all need such a reminder. One benefit of Team In Training is that it allows otherwise healthy adults a healthy connection to the "world" of dying and death. Participants get to know those of all ages and walks of life who have been diagnosed with leukemia or lymphoma. They are reminded that "it" will happen to us all.

Coaches' Inbox: Heartbreak

Coaches,

Just wanted to thank you once more for your coaching, encouragement and training advice. I was very happy with the way the race went and wouldn't hesitate to do that exact race again. I loved it.

And, thank you to the entire staff for being so organized and making each participant feel like we are each the most important person working toward LLS's goals. Your team does a tremendous job.

Sadly and ironically, my efforts to raise money and awareness "in honor of" became a quest "in memory of" when my honored hero passed away on Monday afternoon. I was still in San Diego at the time. He was a great mentor and friend to me, and I will miss him dearly. However, I feel great about the research we are helping to fund through these efforts in his memory.

Thanks again.

Hi Coaches,

My husband passed away yesterday afternoon.
-- Claudia

Dear Claudia,

Our deepest sympathies.

We will never understand the cruelty of this disease – and while we fully understand that our words are inadequate comfort, we hope you will find some solace in our actions. For you & for your beloved husband, we will continue to offer up our legs, our lungs, our hearts.

God bless you, Claudia, in your time of suffering.

Athlete Reflections:
"My Teammates Were There for Me."
– Claudia Garcia, TNT athlete

Claudia's husband Hal was diagnosed with lymphoma in January 2009.

"Hal chose to push the notion of dying out of our daily lives. He never asked from his doctors the precise questions I had, so he never had to hear their answer," Claudia recalled. "His way of dealing with his disease and its progression had many advantages: No mourning at home, we were just dealing with sickness and, hopefully, were going to overcome it. But, it also had a painful drawback. I was left alone with my knowledge, unable to share my anguish with him, the very same one I'd always felt the closest to: my best friend, my husband. The heartbreaking road to widowhood started then.

"So by December 2010, when his end was clearly approaching, my heart was heavy with grief. I felt isolated in my pain, overwhelmed, half dying myself. I needed help. Fast."

Claudia checked into a support group online – but what she read was even more depressing than what she was going through. Then, she found the Team In Training website – and started to sob as she scanned it.

"I attended the first meeting. I can't tell how long it lasted, all I know is that I cried my eyes out. I couldn't say anything; I just listened – and all I was listening to were versions of my own story. I felt understood and supported. Relieved."

So she started training.

"Hal was very proud of me. On an afternoon he was feeling slightly stronger, we went together and got my running shoes. He gave them to me.

"That winter was cold and very rough. But every Saturday morning, as I drove to Lake Zorinsky for our weekly team run, I knew I was doing the only possible thing for me to do: run, experience an effort that helped me imagine what my husband was going through treatment after treatment, believe in my own resilience, build my endurance and fundraise – contributing, even if humbly, to what was helping Hal stay alive."

Claudia could never say much. Choked with emotion, she would run and sob, run and sob.

Hal passed away at the beginning of March 2011.

"My teammates were there for me. More than through their words and their sympathy cards, they were there on the track, helping me complete my half marathon from a place of sharing. At TNT, most of us have been intimately touched by blood cancer.

"I did run the Lincoln Half Marathon. It was an unforgettable experience. I felt really close to Hal, who had been an ocean swimmer and an athlete for most of his adult life until the very end of his strength.

"I felt I had accomplished something for both of us – and that 'something' was bigger than us, went beyond us, somehow easing the pain, and the loss."

After completing the Lincoln Half Marathon, Claudia wrote, "*I was truly overwhelmed with emotion as I was getting into the stadium. I remember when Hal was first diagnosed, he said, "Well, there's nothing to do but get to the other side of the pool," which meant regaining his health. I've thought of those words often. For me, today, crossing that finishing line was about getting to the other side of the pool together. And I had the unexpected pleasure of running with Lindsay, who was one of Hal's nurses (and who I didn't recognize until she re-introduced herself to me). She told me of conversations she'd had with Hal, giving me another new little glimpse of him.*"

Claudia's husband, Andy's father, mothers, friends ... Too many others...

"Coaching marathoners is a challenge; consoling our athletes is a privilege," I told Richard. "It is an integral part of this job – and it is a duty we accept with the greatest of care. The casualties along the way are almost too much to bear, but we know, in our hearts, we are going to beat this disease. We have to. *Keep moving forward.* We say it to our athletes, and, when we are feeling overwhelmed, we say it to ourselves."

Coaches' Inbox:
Heartbreak

Coach,

16 weeks ago, I thought it was a crazy idea that I would be doing a 26.2 mile run. But here we are, and I am going to do it. You were right. The training got me there.

Thanks again for opening my eyes and helping me be a part of something so special. Before we started this, I only knew one person who had ever had leukemia. But in the last two weeks, people very close to me have been affected.

One of my Mom's good friends might lose her life to leukemia.

My brother-in-law has a good friend whose daughter was recently diagnosed with leukemia. And on New Year's Day, my wife's oldest brother was diagnosed with leukemia. So, I will have four names for my jersey... Emma, Maggie, Amelia, and D.R.

As they say, the Lord works in mysterious ways. Thank you again for being there for me and helping me become a part of something so great.

The Battle against Cancer:
On the Front Lines

Meet Joyce Hutchinson, a longtime hospice nurse

What are three things most important to a hospice patient?

First of all, symptom management is very important. When we have pain, we often cannot think of anything else. So, we need to make sure our patients are physically comfortable so they can face what is in front of them.

Another very important item to deal with – the fears the patient experiences. The fear of death is often present, and we want to listen very attentively so that we can help them deal with it or get a clergy person to assist. Another fear is the fear or dread of leaving loved ones behind.

There was a woman I took care of in hospice who had two little girls, 3- and 5-years-old. She was a nurse and was very aware that she was dying but couldn't come to grips with leaving her husband and two little girls behind. She decided to write letters with a gift for each of their eighth grade graduations, high school graduations, wedding days and births of their first babies. Each letter said just what she would say if she were there, and when she completed those, we assisted her in making a mold of her hand. She put a note in each palm that read, "When you get lonesome for your mom, you put your hand in my hand and know that I will be in your heart." She said she was ready now as she was leaving something of herself behind.

The third most important thing to a hospice patient is that we really listen and hear what they have to say or not say. We listen with an ear that tells us if the pain they are complaining of is physical, mental or spiritual pain. We listen with no agenda of our own but to, as much as possible, get into their skin so that we can work to identify where they are and what their needs are.

What are three things that bring hospice patients comfort?
One is for the caregiver to be comfortable with her own mortality. If we learn to confront and accept our own fears, we will become increasingly sensitive to those of the person before us. We will be more compassionate, braver and even clearer in how to enable the dying to understand and face their circumstance themselves.

It is important to help those in our care to have hope. Hope just changes to a more acute kind of hope. Where we might have originally hoped for a cure, we may now hope that we can eat without being sick, be pain free or have peace in our dying. People tend to believe that when they have hospice services that there is no hope. That is not so. The ability to redefine hope is almost limitless.

Another really important aspect that I believe brings comfort to our patients is leaving our agenda at home. We need to be sure that we are always focused on the patient's agenda not ours. It is their journey to death not ours. We need to be able to hear them with no prior judgments, with no expectations of how we would do it. This is especially important in dealing with spirituality. No matter our belief system, we need to walk with them, believing as they do or answering their questions as honestly as we can. Our love for them shows them the love of the eternal, whoever that is for them, more than anything else. Good spiritual care approaches people in these spiritually-charged times with humility and respect, not making assumptions or imposing our agenda. Good spiritual care is gentle. Needing each other is integral to human spirituality. It is in relationship that we make our destiny. It is by working together that dignity in dying is achieved.

What is most important to family members of hospice patients?
First of all, the family wants their loved ones comfortable. It is so very painful for family to see their loved one suffer physical pain. When symptoms are managed, they can get on with other issues.

I think it is important for family members to see that the caregivers are comfortable being with them and their loved one. We can encourage them to be honest with each other and encourage feelings. When we treat the entire situation as a very normal part of this journey here on earth, then it alleviates some of their fear. They often are able to share their feelings, cry together and say things that they have been wanting to say but didn't want to make the other one sad.

I also think humor is important at the bedside and with the family (if it fits the personality of all). Humor brings normalcy to the situation instead of a somber, fearful environment. It is amazing how humor can bring about conversations that would have never have been possible any other way.

What is most difficult for family members of loved ones in hospice care?
Thinking about not having the person in their life or letting them go is very difficult. By listening to the family we allow them to start grieving while the person is still alive – grieving what they will be losing.

I think another very difficult thing for family members is when the patient wants to deny the whole situation or the family wants to shield the patient from the truth with a lot of game playing. First of all, if the patient truly wants to deny that they are dying, we need to allow that as it is their journey. It doesn't seem like the way to go, but it isn't our dying. We need to walk beside them, taking their cues as our guide.

Giving their loved one permission to die is a struggle often, and we help families with that. It is very important if they can give them permission to let go and quit fighting anymore. Once families have the support and know that it is going to happen, they are most always so glad that they told them that is was okay to let go when it was their time. It is a huge relief for the patient as that is often their most painful struggle as they get close to dying.

What is one thing you consistently strive to do as a hospice nurse for each patient?

I strive to be very present to each of my patients and walk with them every step of their journey as they choose to walk it. I strive to make every bit of that journey the best it can be physically, emotionally and spiritually. I believe that it is the greatest of privileges because when someone is dying, it is the only time in our lives that we are bare bones real. There is no need for all of the masks of jealousy, greed and guilt. I strive to show them the God I believe in by my caring, compassion and love.

Nine

HEARTBREAK & HOPE

"Suffering produces endurance, and endurance produces character, and character produces hope. And hope does not disappoint us..." **- Romans 5:3-4**

Part II: Hope

"Do you think we're going to see a cure for cancer in our lifetime?" Richard asked.

"I think some of the best minds in the world are working on it," I said. "I remember sitting in a ballroom in Orlando at an LLS Leadership Conference in early 2012, listening to this brilliant researcher and chemist, Dr. Jay Bradner. I remember thinking, 'I'm looking at the man who's going to cure cancer.' I had chills down my spine. This is a man whose work is funded, in part, by LLS dollars, dollars that TNT athletes – our athletes – raised. The things Dr. Bradner was talking about, the progress they were making at the Dana Farber Cancer Institute and his Bradner Lab. It was..."

I struggled for the right words, "It brought me hope."

I continued, "My intellectual constraints require that I way over-simplify this, but he was telling us about this discovery, this breakthrough they'd made a couple of years prior – a molecular compound that could essentially give cancer cells 'amnesia' and 'trick' them into becoming normal cells. And, you know what they did with this molecule?"

Richard shook his head "no."

"They could have patented it and got rich," I explained. "Instead, they published this structure and shipped samples to labs across the world. Open-source cancer research. The more brilliant minds exploring this avenue, the better. That was their thinking."

I paused. "Every TNT athlete who works to raise research money – and every one of their donors – owns a piece of these breakthroughs. Will there be a cure for cancer in our lifetime? I don't know, but I'm praying for it."

"You're a religious man, Dan?" Richard asked.

"I have my lapses, and I wish my faith was so much stronger, but yes, I would say I am a religious man," I answered. "I believe in God. I believe in Heaven, and I love Jesus and believe he died for my sins. I'm not a theologian; I don't have all the answers; I just know what I feel. You?"

"I went through a very tough time after Cheryl died. I asked all the questions: Why would a loving God allow cancer to exist? Why would He put her – and us – through that? I'm not a perfect man, but we didn't do anything to deserve that. I guess you could say God and I had a falling out."

"And now?"

"We're still working on it" he said.

The conversation drifted for a moment.

"I remember, when my sister was dying," I offered, "sitting with her in the hospital and, through no fault of my own, having the strength and the words to console her. At least I felt like I consoled her. That was God at work. I remember sitting with her in her living room the morning she died, being able to pray the rosary with her during her final hours. That was God at work, carrying me 'Footprints-style.' It was raining that terrible morning, but immediately after Sharon passed, the sun came out. The symbolism blew me away. Her storm was over; she was now in paradise. No more pain. Whole again."

I continued, "Death is hard on the living. But, that ordeal actually strengthened my faith. I saw an outpouring of goodness in others that I'd never seen before. Why did Sharon have to suffer? Why do her two girls and her husband have to suffer? I don't know, but that doesn't mean there isn't an answer. I don't blame God; I just know He was there to console us. By extension, I believe he prepared us for and connected us with Team In Training.

"I remember one of our athletes saying to us, 'This may be a weird question, but do you believe that God is at work in our training?'

"I knew my answer instantly, but I wanted her to expand on her thought. She, then, relayed the story of her rough training week: work was hectic; miles and her overall motivation to train were slipping. She said she was even considering ditching her hopes of running her first full marathon and dialing back to the half.

"That's where, she said, God stepped in. There was no great flash of light or burning bushes. Just a simple text message. For her, God was at work in her training through the care and support of her teammates and mentors. The result was a renewed passion for the task at hand – and one fabulous run."

Athlete Reflections:
"Today Was about Knowing that I Can Finish 26.2."
– Shannon Snow, TNT athlete (from her training blog)

Today was an amazing day!

Even though I am not a morning person, I had made plans to meet my mentor for a Sunday run, and I knew I needed to be there. Carla must have known I needed it too, because at 6 a.m., she sent a text to make sure I was coming. I was... now. I crawled out of bed reluctantly and made my way to Lake Zorinsky.

I was nervous. Carla runs faster than I do, and I have a tendency to burn myself out. But not today. Today, it felt great. Carla pushed me a bit through the first seven miles before she had to leave. At that point, I was in a great place physically and mentally, a great place that I honestly hadn't seen yet this season and certainly not recently.

The truth is – I'd been losing my motivation.

Friday night, I met some friends for dinner; the evening lasted longer than expected; and I missed group training on Saturday morning. This was the second week I had missed without a great excuse and only the third week I've missed total. I was hugely disappointed in myself.

This morning, after three hours and a total of 14 miles, I found my motivation again. And, it all started with Carla and her 6 a.m. text.

Today was a selfish day. It wasn't about cancer; it was about me. Today was about knowing that I can finish 26.2. I needed this run to remind me why I started this – to achieve something I never thought was possible. Today, I learned that I can find my motivation from within; I don't need to depend on my coaches to get me through. Today, I had the run I needed to look forward to the race again, a race which is so much bigger than me.

I continued my deepening conversation with Richard as we continued our descent.

"That question – 'Do you believe God is at work in our training?' – isn't a weird question or a silly question. It is a great question, and I can say without hesitation that my answer is 'yes.'

"One of my most vivid 'God moments' came during a late afternoon run in Omaha's brutal summer heat. I don't remember what I was training for, and I don't remember what compelled me to disregard every good bit of advice I'd heard (and shared) about NOT running in the late afternoon in Omaha's brutal summer heat.

"So there I was on our Keystone Trail, a no frills, no shade, stretch of pavement. It was blazing hot; my water bottle was empty, and I was about a mile from the nearest water fountain.

"And, that's when it happened. Drop... Drop... Drop... Even though the sun was beating down on me and there were precious few clouds in the sky, it started raining on me – washing away my sin of stupidity – and it continued raining on me until I reached that far-off water fountain. And then, like that, it stopped. Did it rain on others as well? I'm pretty sure it did, but, in my mind, God was looking out for a runner who wasn't thinking that day and needed a little cooling help from above.

"I am thankful for that assist and so many others.

"Whether during training or on race day, we always try to remind our athletes to keep an eye out for those miracle moments. More often than not, they are not disappointed."

Miracle Moment:
My Angel Plays Bagpipes
– Kelly McCann, TNT coach/athlete

Kelly's first race in San Diego was in Sharon's honor. Today, a year later, the race was in Sharon's memory, her funeral only four months raw in her memory.

"I had my plan: My training partner would run with me through mile 13, and then my husband, Dan, would jump in for the last half of the race. I had extra salt in my shorts' pocket to help keep my sodium levels in check and prevent cramping, and I knew there was 'Margaritaville' at mile 13 if I needed more. I was ready."

Then, the gun went off – and the battle began.

The first seven miles passed smoothly. Around mile eight, though, the system started to break down. A fierce cramp seized Kelly's gut and slowed her momentum considerably.

"It was miserable," she recalled. "I sent my running partner on; no need for her time to suffer. Besides, I knew Dan and Margaritaville would be waiting for me at 13."

Those next five miles were grueling. Her legs started cramping, and her calves were in a contraction that no amount of stretching could alleviate. (**Lesson learned the hard way** – if you have salt packets in your shorts and you dump water on your head to cool off, the runoff will dissolve those packets into a mushy mess.)

She was broken and clinging to mile 13 in her mind. Dan. Margaritaville.

She did (eventually) make it. Dan didn't.

Devastation.

"I stood in the middle of the street at the corner of our designated spot in disbelief, alone in a crowd of thousands. And that was when I lost it. I was now 'that girl' crying in the middle of the road being passed by sweaty Elvises and people in fishnet bodysuits and superhero and banana costumes. All I could think was, 'I am alone and don't think I can go on.' That's when I heard a voice in my head saying simply 'Go.'"

She had passed the point of no return. It was just as far to go back as it was to go forward. She had no choice but to "Go." One step at a time.

"All I could think was 'right foot...left foot....right....left....' It was a struggle and took all I had (which was barely anything) just to keep up self-propelled forward movement. The sun kept getting hotter and the crowds started to thin. By mile 15, I was looking for a med tent."

Instead, she saw "him."

Ahead, on the side of the road – no crowds– just a lone person standing there. Even amidst the wide variety of people from all walks of life, this person didn't seem to fit in. He wore an old, large brown hat, brown baggy shorts, and a brown ripped shirt. He was a tangle of wild, brown hair and a long beard with a short, round stature. In his hands was a large unidentifiable bag shaped *something*...

"I couldn't tell if he was a spectator, a neighbor, or a homeless man looking for Sunday morning diversion. But he was alone and definitely didn't fit the surroundings."

Was she seeing things?

Then she heard the rumblings of sound – low and drawn out.

Was she hearing things? An auditory hallucination?

Then everything became bright and clear. He came into focus and the item he carried took shape in his hands. It was bagpipes, and Kelly was hearing the beginnings of a song.

"Amazing Grace."

"Sharon's song.... My song..... Straight to my heart from her."

Just four months earlier, on a cold, overcast morning in Dallas, TX, another lone bagpiper had played that same graceful, beautiful melody – as Sharon was laid to rest.

"*...That saved a wretch like me...*"

Once more, Kelly stopped and became "that girl" crying in the middle of the road. But, this time the tears brought release and strength.

In that moment – everything was clear.

She was not alone.

"I knew I would get through this – not because *I* could, but because *we* could. It didn't mean it would be easy, but I knew I would be given the strength to, at least, cross the finish line. And it was the closest I'd felt to Sharon and to God in months.

"Some people say 'God will only give you what you can handle,' but I don't think that is always the case. Sometimes, He gives you *more* than you can handle because that is what encourages you to turn to Him."

Mile 15 gave way to mile 16; mile 16 to 17...

After threatening to "lick" nearby sweating runners for salt, someone took pity on her and gave her half of their packet around mile 21.

At mile 22, she received a tap on the shoulder and a warm greeting from a familiar voice. "Hey beautiful."

Dan did eventually make it to their mile 13 meeting spot, delayed, as it turned out, by a race morning trolley snafu. Certain he'd missed his wife; he just started running from there.

"How he found me in that mass of athletes – nine miles later – I don't know, but we were able to finish that unforgettable race – amazing grace – side by side."

By the way, Kelly's running partner, who finished ahead of her, never saw the bagpipe player. Her teammates, who finished after her, say they remembered seeing a "homeless-looking guy" around mile 15, but he wasn't playing anything...

Miracle Moment:
Pennies from Heaven
– Kristi Kempkes, TNT athlete

A penny may seem pretty insignificant these days. By themselves, they have no real buying power. Even banding together, it takes about 300 of them to equal a simple gallon of gas. But, on that June morning on that half marathon course in San Diego, CA, a single penny was priceless.

Kristi's grandfather passed away in June 2010 a year before that race. (Actually, if you want to get technical about it, he was her step-grandfather, but she never doubted that he loved her like she was descendent of his own flesh and blood. "My girl" – that's what he wrote on the back of her senior picture that he kept in his bible.)

"I have so many memories of spending time at my grandparents' house near the railroad tracks and of my grandfather pursuing one of his favorite hobbies: coin collecting," Kristi recalled. "I remember leaving work after learning of his death, having to stop at a gas station fill up. As I was getting out of the car, I looked down (something I don't normally do), and there, on the ground, was a penny. I took it as a comforting sign. He was with me."

The next day, a friend took Kristi out to lunch. Upon getting out of the car, she spotted another penny on the ground. Another sign.

Now, fast forward to the San Diego Rock 'N Roll Half Marathon a year later and two weeks shy of the anniversary of his death.

"I was struggling big-time on the course and was in a lot of pain. Miles of walking on a tilt – like walking across the side of a hill – had taken a toll. I hadn't trained for anything like that."

Her coach found her with about four miles to go, and, as they walked together, the coach spotted something – a "lucky" penny on the ground.

"I began to tear up. When she asked if I was okay, I told her the story of my grandfather and the pennies. 'I don't ever look down at the ground,' my coach said. 'I can go back and get it… It was back there by the railroad tracks.'

"At that point, I began to cry because I KNEW he was with me still. 'My grandparent's use to live by the railroad tracks,' I told her."

It was enough to give the coach goose bumps. From that moment on, Kristi knew she would finish the half-marathon.

"I would finish in honor of a family friend who was in remission from lymphoma. And, I would finish for and with my grandfather who was there with me during a very difficult time, surrounding me with strength and signs and unconditional love from Heaven!"

Two powerful forces pushing her through to the end. Two powerful forces – and a penny.

"That little copper coin may seem pretty insignificant these days, but in San Diego that June morning, it bought me a personal moment of inspiration I will never forget."

Miracle Moment:
A Short Rest – and a Little Prayerful Intervention
– Andi Mucklow, TNT athlete

On September 12, 2010, Andi woke up in our nation's capital with one goal in mind – finish the Nation's Triathlon with Team In Training. But, as the start of her race drew closer, doubt started to creep in: "What the heck was I thinking when I signed up for this event?" she thought. "I can't swim this distance!"

She felt herself shiver. She wasn't cold; she was scared to death.

When the announcer called for her wave to enter the Potomac River, Andi steadied her nerves and jumped in, thinking of only one thing – **COURTNEY**, her honored hero.

"What if she had said, 'I can't do this; leukemia is too hard. I can't take chemotherapy any more. I am scared.' Giving up was not an option for my wonderfully strong, amazing niece, and it was not an option for me," Andi recalled.

The air-horn sounded. Andi tucked chin to chest and started to swim. Before she knew it, she was 400 meters out, sight-checking every so often to make sure she was on course.

"I kept singing to myself like Dory from *Finding Nemo*: 'Just keep swimming, just keep swimming. What do we do? We swwwimmmm...'"

The calming effect of the singing only last so long.

As she approached 900 meters, her asthma started to act up.

"I needed my inhaler. I didn't have it in the water," she said. "I swam to the nearest kayak with a lifeguard (one of many out there to support the swimmers), all the while praying I would be able to calm my breathing enough to finish the swim – and the race."

As Andi reached for the edge of the kayak, the lifeguard asked if she was okay. She told him she was asthmatic but with a short rest, she would be fine.

A short rest – and a little prayerful intervention.

Would you believe there was one other athlete holding on to the kayak – also an asthmatic – and he offered Andi his inhaler? The exact type that she used.

"I prayed for relief," she said. "God answered."

After a huff on the inhaler, Andi pushed on to the swim exit – and, ultimately, an overall tri finish of 3:44:24 (just 36 seconds short of the 3:45 max time she was allowing herself).

"When will I stop these races and end my journey with LLS? When we all cross that ultimate finish line and find a cure. Until then, I will continue to swim, bike and run.

"I will continue to raise money and awareness.

"And, I will continue to fight with Courtney."

Team In Training Spotlight:
"You Just Have to Keep Fighting"
– The David Gong Story,
in his own words

A devastating accident could have thrust David Gong into an irreversible whirlpool of depression and despair. Instead, the TNT alum serves as an inspiration, a testament to the resilience of the human spirit and our ability to fight through herculean challenges.

The week before going to Alaska, I remember thinking, "God, do I really want to do this? I am just so tired." I had done the Ironman and the Rock 'n' Roll Marathon a few weeks before. Plus, I had just moved from a one-bedroom condo into a house that I had rented out for five or six years. But, I had put this trip together to do the Mount Marathon Race, and 18 other people were going. I couldn't not go.

The Mount Marathon Race is the longest-running race in the U.S. next to the Boston Marathon. It started in the early 1900's. People come from all of the states to race it, and you have to register early because it is really restricted at the top.

The Mount Marathon Race® is an annual footrace featuring a climb and descent on Mt. Marathon (3,022 feet in elevation). Participants race a mile and a half up and a mile and a half down, including cliffs, scree fields, waterfalls, and a spectacular view. Runners from around the world are drawn to this signature event. -- cmdev.seward.com

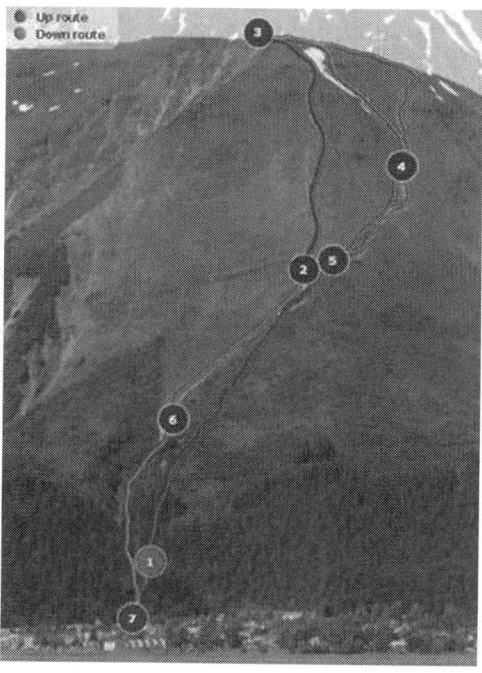

I always liked climbing mountains. When you get to the top, if you get up there alone, it's just such a cool feeling, to be able to look around and see things all by yourself.

That was my goal that day – climb as fast as I could so I could get that extra minute or two by myself. I still remember that 360-degree view. You look out over what's called Resurrection Bay. You see those mountains just come right to the ocean. They are snow covered still, and it's June. People don't realize just how steep it is. 3000 ft. That's a hell of climb in like an hour or two.

That Wednesday after the race, a group of us went to climb the mountain again. We had to check out that morning so we only had a couple of hours. I thought, "I know half these people aren't going to make it up," and I remember warning them about how dangerous it was: "Guys, you have to be really careful here. It's really steep."

I wound up taking a group of five to the top. I was really flying. I love that feeling, that burning in your lungs. Your heart is at its maximum rate, and you are putting what you can into it. I made it to the top maybe five minutes before everyone else. You just stop, look around, reflect a little bit, and you go, "Wow!"

To get down the mountain, we had to take a chute. I could tell the others were scared. I saw the look in their eyes, and they weren't saying anything. I thought, "Okay, we're kind of in trouble now because they don't want to go down the chute. I'm not going to force them to go down the chute."

I walked maybe 10 feet, and then I heard this big scream. It wasn't like a terrifying scream; it was more like somebody on a roller coaster. One of the girls had jumped into the chute. I told the others, "I've got to go in now. I have to make sure she is okay. You guys can follow behind me."

I didn't think. I just jumped in. Now, I'm in the chute, and I wanted to go really fast to catch up because she was maybe 10 seconds ahead of me. I'm flying down, not controlling my speed, trying to catch up to her. At that point, she gets scared but does the right thing and just stops dead in the chute. So now I'm flying down and all of the sudden, I'm like, "Oh crap, I'm going to plow into her." I was going pretty fast, maybe 20 miles an hour.

I see her and instinctively think, "Just go to the right." It kind of slopes up a little bit, which I thought was good, maybe that would slow me down. I came right up on her, just tapped her a little bit but immediately went to the right. She was kind of laughing; we were both kind of laughing. As I went to the right, I was looking at her, and I didn't realize it – but there was a big cliff just a few feet away.

I crossed that edge. At that point, it was just solid ice on the side. I remember sliding down, trying to dig my hands in, but there's nothing to dig in and you're going faster and faster. You know it's not going to go forever; you know there's going to be rocks eventually. It was like falling out of a building, knowing that you are going to hit the ground.

I hit the rocks and started getting hit in the head. My feet were kicking the rocks up in front of me. I was trying to use my hands to stop, which meant there was really no way to cover my face. Rocks are just flying like they are being shot out of a cannon, and they are all hitting me in the head. One really clocked me bad. I almost got knocked out. Then, I remember going up in the air and coming straight down on that rock, almost like a spike.

That is what broke my backbone in half and severed my spinal cord.

I knew right away. Once I finally stopped, I knew I couldn't move.

My lungs were collapsing, and it got really hard to talk. I knew my life was in danger. Blood was coming out my ears and nose. I couldn't open my eyes.

People started making their way to me. I could tell something was very wrong because they weren't saying anything. I said, "I can't move. I think I broke my back."

I heard them in the background: "He's dying. We have to get the helicopter up here!"

Turns out all of the helicopters were deployed because of a big forest fire. We didn't know when we'd be able to get one.

A climber, who was also an EMT, offered what aid he could and called an ambulance. The ambulance folks climbed part of the mountain and said, "We can't make it. We're not going to climb the rest of the way."

So, you're just kind of there for a couple of hours.

I remember going in and out of consciousness. It's cold and chaotic; people are crying. I can't really talk much anymore because my lungs have completely collapsed, and I'm just grasping for air.

It wasn't like my life flashed before me. People always think that you see some bright light like in the movies. It was really just like going to sleep. That is what it felt like almost.

I could hear the helicopter. I remember them putting me on a sled and how painful it was just being moved. I remember being in that helicopter and being in the emergency room, waking up a little bit. Doctors rushing around. My whole chest cavity now was filled with blood.

When the doctors put the first chest tube in, all I heard was, "Oh my God!" There was this big rush of air. It's like your lungs are just waiting to inflate. They're getting all this pressure off. The blood, it just went everywhere. The doctors were looking around just kind of stunned at how much blood was trapped inside the chest cavity.

I flew by helicopter back to Anchorage and the main hospital that night. I was kind of in and out of consciousness when my neurologist came in, but I said right to him, "Am I going to walk again?"

"Can you open your eyes a little?" he said. "I want to show you something."

He showed me my x-rays and said, "There is just no way you're ever going to walk again. There is no way your spinal cord survived this kind of a break."

And then he just kind of walked out. Just like that.

My brother called shortly after, and I remember telling him, "Look, be careful how you tell Mom." She was 70 years old, and she had been through this before. My sister was killed in a car accident when she was 16. So, for my Mom to get another call like that, I just knew it would devastate her. She didn't deserve that.

A couple of days later, after my breathing had stabilized, they did a surgery. My mother did come from Indiana, and my brother flew up from San Diego. Before operating, the staff told me, "You have maybe a 30-40 percent chance of not surviving because your lungs have been so damaged."

Before they put you under, you're like, "Okay, well, this might be that last time I'm awake."

I remember I was so happy when I did wake up.

The week after was real bad though. I got pneumonia from all of the trauma to the lungs. It's almost like you're drowning, you can't breathe. You can't sleep; you've got fever and all these tubes in you still. You can't eat, and you realize you're going to be paralyzed for the rest of your life. All these things are hitting you, and then the mental depression sets in.

Being paralyzed, it's more than not being able to move your legs. You've also lost your core muscles, all those things medically that they don't really tell you about, but you start to figure out. "How am I going to do this? How am I going to do that?"

Then it starts to hit home. You know you are never going to have the same life again. You're just lying in a hospital bed; you can't really do anything. You have a lot of time to think about it. That was the hard part.

Going through rehab was also tough. You're depressed. A lot of people want to see you, but you don't want them to see you in this condition. It would be different if you could say I'm looking forward to getting out; I'm going to do all these things. But you know it's permanent; you aren't going to get any better.

I would see pictures of me running. You know you're not going to have that kind of life anymore. You know gradually that those friends aren't going to be able to share the same things the friendship was kind of built on, like running and hiking.

Your mind is telling you – they are not going to want to hang around you very much longer. You realize that you're going to lose a lot of the things you enjoy; all of your dreams are never going to happen. There's just a lot of grief with that.

I remember some of the people I was in the hospital with, like this one guy who was 28 year old. His injuries were a little lower than mine.

I was out by the bay in my wheelchair one day, saw his sister and asked, "How's your brother?" She told me he had killed himself about a month earlier. She didn't want to tell me because she wanted everybody to stay positive.

Then there was this ex-Marine who was in a motorcycle accident, a real low injury. He could walk a little bit. I saw him at a race like two years later in a hand cycle. I remember telling him about those hand cycles because I had worked with challenged athletes. In 2008, he went on to win a gold medal in Beijing in the hand cycle race at the Paralympics. He just won a bronze in London. He is one of the best hand cyclers in the world now.

Believe it or not, he can do a marathon course in about an hour. So, that's about 26 miles an hour in a hand cycle. That's pretty amazing. So you just see the two worlds that people can go into, you can either make it or you don't.

"I made it through, but I'm still fighting."

Though he doesn't like to speak about it, David lives in near constant pain. Still, he is moving forward. He is making it. After an intensive period of rehabilitation, he took to hand cycling himself.

Hand cycling is enjoyable because you are outdoors, you are moving. It's like riding a bicycle again. You can imagine you are out running. I'd love to just get out on the road and go forever, just keep riding. Even though it's painful, it is one of those things that is way worth it to do. Still, I can only do it maybe six months out of the year because it's hard to get people to help.

That's the good thing about Team In Training. It's always there, and those are the people who help every Saturday. They are very compassionate and giving, and they are the kind of people who react well to those in tough situations.

Team In Training, that's why I've kept doing it. It's one part of my life that hasn't been taken away. I am fortunate for that. I find a lot of inspiration from the honored heroes, too.

I remember about a year after I got hurt, there was this honored hero, maybe 16 or 17 years old. She wanted to come to this party, to this fundraiser because the whole team was training for her. It meant a lot to her. I saw her family help her in, and it was clear that she was just really tired and weak.

Her parents said they tried to talk her out of coming to that party, that it would be too risky. But, she told them she wanted to go out on a Saturday night, get dressed up, maybe for the last time, and be with friends. I think she died a month later.

And then there was one girl, a few years ago, who was diagnosed with leukemia two months before she was supposed to run the Rock 'n' Roll Marathon in San Diego. She actually came back and talked to us about a year ago. It was very inspiring to see that.

Things like that really stick in your mind, people fighting through challenges. I look at life now as you just have to keep fighting through whatever happens. In everybody's life, there are going to be those challenges. You just have to deal with them.

The Next Event

I'll probably do the Rock 'n Roll Marathon again. Training starts in January. I haven't been on my hand cycle since May or June. I'm looking forward to it.

Things with the Team, I can't say enough about how positive they are. A lot of it is the cause, but a lot of it is the people you meet. There's always somebody each season that becomes a good friend. I think that is one of the best things about the Team, you have these two big benefits: you are meeting these people that you wouldn't have met otherwise, and you are doing something great for the cause. You may not really realize it all the time, but you are saving lives. I'm just looking forward to the day when all cancer is cured. Whether it's five, ten or more years from now, it will be a cool feeling to know that you had a part in that.

An Update on David

David completed the Rock 'n Roll Marathon that he mentioned in his interview. In the time since, he has won the Leukemia & Lymphoma Society's 2013 Man of the Year award and completed another Rock 'n Roll Marathon with Team In Training. David is one of only 80 people who have completed every Rock 'n Roll San Diego Marathon! This brings David's total funds raised for LLS to over $110,000 since he first joined 16 years ago.

David Gong and Judy Mansisidor at the finish of the 2013 San Diego Rock 'n Roll Marathon

The Battle against Cancer: On the Front Lines

Venture Philanthropy

Venture Philanthropy, as defined by the National Venture Capital Association, "applies venture capital strategies, skills, and resources to charitable giving. It focuses on leadership, bold ideas, developing strong teams, active board involvement, and long-term investment."[11]

Through its venture philanthropy efforts, the Leukemia & Lymphoma Society is distinguished and uniquely competitive in the development of new drug therapies to accelerate therapies and cures for leukemia, lymphoma and myeloma patients. In addition to providing academic grants at the university level, LLS channels donated funds

---

[11] www.nvca.org

to promising researchers and developing companies through two of its innovative programs: the Targets, Leads and Candidates program, "a novel approach to venture philanthropy partnerships with the pharmaceutical industry," and the Therapy Acceleration Program.

Therapy Acceleration Program or TAP

"The LLS Therapy Acceleration Program (TAP) is a strategic initiative to speed the development of blood cancer treatments and supportive diagnostics. TAP looks to fund projects related to therapies that have the potential to change the standard of care for patients with blood cancer, especially in areas of high unmet medical need.

TAP funding assists both clinical investigators and companies in gaining critical proof of concept data that better enables them to obtain the resources they need or a partner to complete the testing, registration and marketing of new treatments for leukemia, lymphoma and myeloma," including a promising new therapy for multiple myeloma, ACY-1215.[12]

Multiple Myeloma Outcomes

The outcomes for multiple myeloma patients have improved significantly in recent years. The five-year survival rate has increased from 12% in 1960-1963 (whites) to 41.1% from 2001-2007 (for all races and ethnicities).[13]

While the progress in survival is significant, there is more work to be done.

What follows is an examination of LLS's Therapy Acceleration Program and the genesis of ACY-1215 from the perspective of three key players:

- The founding university researcher of ACY-1215, Dr. Ken Anderson, Director of the Jerome Lipper Multiple Myeloma

---

[12] www.lls.org
[13] "LLS Facts" publication, 2012

Center and Lebow Institute for Myeloma Therapeutics at the Dana-Farber Cancer Institute
- Walter Ogier, President and Chief Executive Officer of Acetylon Pharmaceuticals, Inc., a recently-formed company that hopes to bring ACY-1215 to market
- Mark Alles, President and Chief Operating Officer at Celgene Corporation, a significant investor in Acetylon Pharmaceuticals

Meet Dr. Ken Anderson, one of two scientific founders on the Board of Directors at Acetylon Pharmaceuticals Inc.

Talk to us about the biology behind histone deacetylase (HDAC) inhibitors, specifically ACY-1215, or Ricolinostat? How do they battle against myeloma?

Multiple myeloma (MM) is a cancer that produces excess monoclonal protein in association with too many plasma cells in the bone marrow. So that's the hallmark: excess bone marrow plasma cells and the protein monoclonal they produce either in the blood and/or urine.

Over the years, the prognosis of MM has markedly improved. This is a consequence of understanding the importance of the tumor in its microenvironment, which is the bone marrow.

The new treatments work against the tumor cell and in the microenvironment. One of the original new classes of drugs that has been developed and approved over the last decade is called Bortezomib, a proteasome inhibitor. Proteasome inhibitors block the breakdown of proteins in a garbage disposal, the proteasome. Since MM cells make large amounts of excess protein, inhibiting their ability to breakdown this protein, causes them to fill up with their own protein, and commit suicide.

How has LLS directly assisted with the development of ACY-1215?

The Leukemia & Lymphoma Society has a wonderful program called TAP (Therapy Acceleration Program). Acetylon applied to TAP for some financial assistance for the purpose of rapidly moving this promising medicine, ACY-1215 or Ricolinostat, into patients for the first time and into clinical trials. We showed that ACY-1215 blocked the aggresome garbage disposal, and that Bortezomib, to inhibit the proteasome, together with ACY-1215 to block the aggresome, triggered synergistic MM cell death.

In my view, this program is highly innovative, fills a very import unmet medical need and makes science count for patients. TAP makes it possible to take a very promising lead in the laboratory into first- in-man clinical trials. As a consequences, this program is a wonderful model of how to work together to foster progress.

The assistance is given to new companies that are trying to bring forward highly-innovative medicines for blood diseases and cancers. TAP is very selective and rigorously based on data. In other words, only the most promising leads are being chosen for early support.

If these drugs are successful, the LLS recovers their generous support. The investment that they've made then comes back to them so that they can further invest in research and all the other wonderful things that they do. Their assistance is invaluable, and in many cases, these drugs simply would not go forward were it not for LLS.

A Natural Partnership

Acetylon and LLS work together; it's a natural partnership. From the laboratory-investigators reporting the findings – to the clinical-investigators who are doing the clinical trials – they are all working together with LLS, all on the same team. It's a wonderful concept. And it facilitates formation of the teams needed.

I'm a huge supporter of LLS. My trainees and I have been funded by their efforts in the past. They have been a major force in the advancements that have been made in the diagnosis, prognosis and treatment of blood diseases and, in particular, blood cancers.

How does TAP develop findings that otherwise might move no further than a research laboratory?
TAP says, "Okay, we have a new promising finding. We are going to try to bridge that gap from the bench to the bedside and make sure that,

it can be tested in clinical trials." It's very natural, it's very innovative and, ultimately, it's going to be hugely successful, in my opinion, because:
1. There undoubtedly will be new medicines that come out as a consequence.
2. The program will ultimately sustain itself because successful medicines will provide funds back to LLS from those efforts and allow them to then fund the next generation of new medicines.

It is a win-win.

Meet Walter Ogier, Co-founder, President and Chief Executive Officer, Acetylon Pharmaceuticals Inc.

Can you explain your relationship with LLS, particularly the funding Acetylon received through TAP and how it has helped move the development of Ricolinostat (ACY-1215) forward?

Our company, Acetylon, was founded, as a lot of small start-up pharmaceutical or biotech companies are founded, based on a limited amount of investment from angel investors, private individuals rather than venture.

We had plans to develop a clinical program in multiple myeloma, but we didn't have the funding in place to be able to advance that effort into the clinic and actually begin the clinical trials. Then, LLS became interested in our program and, after learning more about what we were planning to do, decided that this would be a program that would be appropriate for their Therapy Accelerator Program.

That actually helped us very much in bringing together further investment from the same types of private individuals, some of whom are cancer patients, some of whom have a strong interest in seeing new therapies advance into clinical trials and beyond. So, we were able to bring together the balance of the money to be able to carry that program forward.

LLS Played a Key Role

LLS played a key role for us in giving some validation of the concept, and the amount of money that they put in was really quite significant. They initially came in with about $5 million in funding and just recently have increased it to $6 million.

The clinical trial is divided into three phases:
- Phase Ia is a very traditional dose escalation study involving increasing doses of our drug candidate ACY -1215 as a monotherapy or as a single agent. Patients would have either relapsed or relapsed refractory multiple myeloma.
- Phase 1b combines our drug candidate ACY-1215 with two standard-of-care drugs for treating myeloma: the drug Velcade, or Bortezomib, which is marketed by Takeda Millennium Pharmaceuticals, and a generic drug called dexamethasone. That also involves an escalation of our drug in terms of dosing alongside of the label dosing of the other two drugs.
- If and when we reach the tolerated dose of the combination of the drugs and we are seeing patients respond at a satisfactory level, we will move to phase 3, adding an additional 55 total patients to the trial in order to approach statistical significance in the overall result from the trial.

Do you know of any other programs like TAP? Dr. Anderson seems to think this is very unique.

I think LLS has been one of the pioneers, if not the pioneer, in doing this financial arrangement for cancer research. Clinical trials can be very expensive, and many nonprofit organizations don't try to fund clinical trial work. They fund things at earlier stages, bench research or things like that, where a smaller amount of money can have a substantial impact.

You know it costs. Clinical trials for drug development tend to become more expensive as the phases of a trial increase, as the number of patients involved in each phase increases. A typical cancer drug will be given to 1000 patients or more before FDA approval is given. It can become very expensive. So, it is important to have funding, particularly in the early stages, where venture capital funding has become harder to obtain.

Another company that has partnered with LLS and has also partnered and funded with you is Celgene. Talk about that relationship.

Celgene is quite a bit larger company than we are and already has some very successful drugs on the market. Celgene's relationship with us is actually quite unusual. They invested a substantial amount of equity in our company, $15 million in total, at the beginning of calendar year 2012, but they did it without any strings attached. We have not had to give away any of the marketing rights that we have available for our drug. So, it's a relatively early investment by a large pharmaceutical company, and it is further helping to fund additional clinical development. One of the things we've been able to do with the funding is to begin to pair our lead drug, ACY-1215, with other drugs that are currently being used to treat multiple myeloma.

There's certainly the possibility that Celegene will, in some future transaction or funding event with us, be interested in acquiring marketing rights to our drug, but so far, we haven't gone down that path with them. Our expectation is that there will be other companies interested in that at some point in time. There is also the possibility that we will remain independent develop the drug ourselves through the clinical phase and to market.

I think the relationship Celgene has with LLS is very interesting also. It is a case of a for-profit company working with a nonprofit institution to find ways to develop promising new therapies into clinical development. Celgene has an indirect interest in seeing that succeed, but I think the relationship between those two companies is really pioneering for the field. My hope is that it will continue to be useful for new companies as they are looking for ways to bridge that funding gap.

Meet Mark Alles, President and Chief Operating Officer, Celgene Corporation, in his own words

Acetylon's Innovation

The biotech industry is still the most innovative part of healthcare across the board. As an incubator of ideas for the treatment of rare orphan diseases, cancers in particular, biotechnology companies are still the engine driving a lot of innovation and understanding.

The other overlap between Celgene and Acetylon is multiple myeloma, which is a rare blood cancer. This area is really why Celgene has become a global biotechnology powerhouse. We have multiple drugs for the treatment of multiple myeloma starting with thalidomide, Revlimid (Lenalidomide) and now we are soon to get, we hope, FDA approval for another drug called pomalidomide for myeloma.

ACY-1215

The lead compound that Acetylon is working on is a drug called ACY-1215 (Ricolinostat), and so we are doing combination studies, for example, with ACY-1215 and Revlimid for multiple myeloma.

It starts with disease categories where there is an overlap in research and potentially commercialization, and then these partnerships emerge that often times involve licensing deals or direct investments. In the case of Celgene with Acetylon, we've made a direct investment in the company and, as an investor, have certain rights and are working on novel combination studies to help them and our portfolio.

LLS's Targets, Leads and Candidates Program

We have also made an investment in LLS through the Targets, Leads and Candidates Program, where they are looking for opportunities to partner with companies.

LLS will screen drugs through their scientific efforts and give us the opportunity to make new investments or come up with ideas for companies or drugs that we might invest in.

We like that partnership with LLS. We like the idea of making a general contribution to LLS and then of having the relationship with them to identify new drugs and new start-up companies.

LLS serves a purpose beyond advocacy. They can connect science with companies and accelerate drug development in a very innovative way.

The Battle against Cancers

Many companies are doing what Celgene is trying to do, trying to find new weapons, new drugs, new targets to fight cancer. It's interesting now that the word "target" is used. We are looking for "targeted therapies" or personal therapies, these are words that have meaning for patients.

When we talk about the war against cancer or myeloma, 10 years ago when I started at Celgene, the median survival for a patient who got treated with all the therapies, including a stem cell transplant, was about two-and-half to three years.

Today, if someone is diagnosed with multiple myeloma and they are able to get access to all these modern therapies, the median survival is approaching nine years, so a tripling of survival in less than ten years for a cancer that is incurable.

It is a war, literally, against cancer. Terms like "battle," "fight", and "target" are appropriate for these diseases – and most important for the kids. When you have kids fighting these battles, it is really important for the parents and the families to grab onto that language. It gives a sense of control in a circumstance where really, the sense of control can be lost.

I know so many doctors, nurses and social workers who have dedicated their lives to helping people with cancer and who take it personally. I am honored to be working with them.

An Update on the LLS Relationship with Acetylon (courtesy of an LLS/Acetylon press release):

The Leukemia & Lymphoma Society and Acetylon Pharmaceuticals Partner to Advance the Clinical Development of Acetylon's Ricolinostat (ACY-1215) Drug Candidate for Multiple Myeloma

- Funding Will Support the First Clinical Trial of a Class II-Selective Next Generation HDAC Inhibitor

WHITE PLAINS, New York and BOSTON, Massachusetts, May 11, 2011 -- The Leukemia & Lymphoma Society (LLS) and Acetylon Pharmaceuticals today announced a newly formed business alliance whereby Acetylon and LLS will jointly support a Phase I/II clinical trial of Acetylon's oral selective HDAC6 inhibitor drug candidate, ACY-1215, in multiple myeloma. LLS has committed to provide up to $4.85 million in milestone-trenched funding to Acetylon, and a joint clinical oversight committee will be formed. Acetylon is focused on the discovery and development of potential drug candidates based on next-generation Class II-selective HDAC inhibitors.
www.acetylon.com
www.lls.org

An Update on the Acetylon Relationship with Celgene Corporation:

In 2011, LLS partnered with Acetylon Pharmaceuticals, Inc. to accelerate the development of a novel treatment for multiple myeloma. The innovative nature of this project was recognized in fiscal year 2013 when Celgene Corporation signed a $100 million agreement to further develop Acetylon's group of HDAC6-selective histone deacetylase (HDAC) inhibitors. In this case, the large pharmaceutical company and the public market recognized the promise of a new therapy being supported by LLS by making significant additional investments. These investments enable our biotechnology partners to overcome risk thresholds and move promising new treatments forward.[14]

What follows is text from official press release announcing Celegene's additional investment in Acetylon since these interviews were completed:

---

[14] http://www.lls.org/content/nationalcontent/pdf/LLS_2013_AR.pdf

Acetylon Pharmaceuticals and Celgene Corporation Announce an Exclusive Strategic Collaboration to Advance the Science of Epigenetics
- Strategic Collaboration Includes Option for Celgene to Acquire Acetylon

BOSTON – July 29, 2013 – Acetylon Pharmaceuticals, Inc., the leader in development of selective histone deacetylase (HDAC) inhibitors for enhanced therapeutic outcomes (the "Company"), today announced a strategic collaboration and option agreement with Celgene Corporation (NASDAQ: CELG), which supports the development of Acetylon's portfolio of oral, selective HDAC inhibitors in oncology, hematology, immunology, and neurologic disease indications. The agreement includes an exclusive option for the future acquisition of Acetylon by Celgene.

The collaboration will focus on the continued clinical advancement of Acetylon's lead candidate, ACY-1215, an oral first-in-class selective HDAC6 inhibitor being developed for hematological malignancies, ACY-738 for neurological diseases, an HDAC1/2 inhibitor, and a yet unnamed project, spanning cancer and non-cancer disease indications. Under the terms of the agreement, Acetylon will receive a $100 million upfront cash payment. In return, Celgene receives an exclusive option to acquire Acetylon at a cash purchase price that will be within a defined value range and based upon future independent valuations of Acetylon. Acetylon will retain control of its drug development programs during the option period. If Celgene exercises its option to acquire Acetylon, an upfront payment determined from the valuation process and subject to a minimum of $500 million will be paid at the time of closing. Additionally, Acetylon shareholders will be eligible to receive potential future milestone payments for either approvals or additional indications of drugs developed by Acetylon and for accomplishing defined sales targets. If all the milestones are achieved, the additional value accruing to Acetylon shareholders would be $1.1 billion, comprised of $250 million for regulatory milestones and $850 million for sales milestones.

www.acetylon.com
www.celegene.com

Ten

Event Weekend

"We actually got our official race jersey this week and it is all feeling pretty real now. If I think about it too much, I start getting nervous. Nine days now for us. Just a few miles this week to keep loose and then we are off to the races. Thanks to everyone for their support. We feel very proud and blessed to represent you all in this race to find a cure. Next update... Phoenix!" – **Scott J. McCoid, TNT athlete (from his training blog)**

Civilization began to come into view as our plane continued its descent. California homes. Cars. Life in a complicated world. The flight attendant made her final pass, collecting trash, checking lap belts, making sure the cabin was in the process of shutting down all electronic devices.

"With all that build up and hard work, I imagine actually making it to your race is something else," Richard said.

"These event weekends are the reward," I said. "Our athletes have spent months training in all conditions, fundraising and otherwise upending their lives. It's not like they're sponsored. They have jobs and families and lives. Event weekend is their thank you, their victory lap."

I continued, "This is my eighth trip to San Diego as either a spectator, athlete or coach. Kelly ran her first TNT event here – the San Diego Rock-n-Roll Marathon in June of 2004. I'll never forget it. At the 'Inspiration Dinner' the night before the race, we were greeted by the most glorious, joyful noise. What seemed like hundreds of coaches, mentors and TNT staff members lined the route into the convention center ballroom – clapping, shouting, blowing horns and ringing cowbells. The red carpet. A hero's welcome. I felt guilty soaking up the adulation (I hadn't trained or fundraised at that point), but, I admit, I loved it. I knew I wanted some of that for myself – for real.

"A year later at my first TNT event, the Ford New York City Triathlon, the red carpet wasn't quite as wild and the dinner crowd paled in comparison to the thousands in San Diego, but I'll never forget that evening. My family was there to support me – my mom and dad, my brother and his wife. Kelly. A picture of Sharon popped up on the screen as part of a video tribute to all of our honored heroes. The tears were instant – and cathartic."

I added, "I won't deny there is a measure of personal glory in what we do; crossing the finish line is amazing. But, in the end, what sets the Team In Training athlete apart is our true motivation – sacrificing our time, our effort, our bodies in hopes of a world without cancer.

"The Inspiration Dinner brings that all home. Speakers talk openly and emotionally about their triumphs and their losses. Tears flow. The desire to run grows. Hold on. Just a few more hours...

"I had the privilege of speaking at a couple of inspiration dinners before the Des Moines Marathon. I am not a public person – nor am I a public speaker – but when duty called, I took my turn at the podium:

Like a playground bully, Cancer kicks us when we're down and spits at us: 'Have you had enough yet?'

Absolutely, we've had enough.

Are we ready to give up?

Never.

When it comes to bullies, we have two choices: we can fight or we can run.

Team in Training allows all of us to do both.

So tomorrow, here in Des Moines, Iowa, we will fight and we will run.

We will wear our purple with pride; we will push through the fatigue; we will never give in – never, never, never, never (Winston Churchill) – and we will deal with the consequences of our insanity on Monday.

Baseball legend Roberto Clemente said, "If we have a chance to make a difference in this world – and we don't – then we are wasting our time."

You are making a difference; we are making a difference.

We are all in this together. We will find a cure one day, and when we do, you can take pride knowing that you played a crucial part.

May God bless you all for that – and may God bless the people you're running for tomorrow!

----- **Original Message** -----
From: Your Team In Training Coaches
Hey Team,

It is, indeed, coming down to the wire – almost time to collect the reward for all of your hard work! Think back to that information meeting you attended months ago. Now, think about how far you've come since then. Amazing!

We have no doubt you all are going to succeed on Sunday, and you're going to do it in fine fashion.

God bless and Go Team!

Athlete's Journey:
Shambra L. Clifford's Story – Part III

The flight to San Francisco was charged with excitement. Shambra and her teammates had been training together for months – and it was all about to pay off. The pre-race Inspiration Dinner only enhanced the electricity.

"We all wore our Team In Training jackets that we earned by reaching our fundraising goal. As we walked over from our hotel, we heard shouting, pounding, and bells," Shambra recalled. "The noise grew stronger as we got closer. We turned the corner and saw coaches and mentors from all chapters lined up cheering for us as we walked into the building. It must have been about a mile of people cheering for us as we walked through.

"All the training and hard work we put into getting to this moment brought tears to my eyes and a burst of memories through my mind: the struggles my brother endured as well as the other patients I met throughout his treatments. This was an amazing surprise, and` it was then that I realized even more the importance of this organization. It was a beautiful site, and I was deeply grateful to be a part of something filled with such love."

----- Original Message -----
From: Your Team In Training Coaches
Hey Team,

Despite all the nervousness and the swirl and all the information we're throwing at you, we never want you to lose sight of one thing: This is going to be FUN, a weekend where you spend time with other strong men and women, rewarding yourselves for a job well done. On Sunday morning, we're going to take a few hours out of this phenomenal, fun weekend to take care of some business.

The race will start – as scheduled – at 7a.m. no matter how much you worry about it. Once the gun goes off, you are committed to crossing the starting line and, after that, you have just one assignment -- keep... moving... forward... (The dozens of emails we've sent over the months – the tens of thousands of words... all the discussions... it all boils down to that... Keep moving forward... Let it be your race day mantra...)

Be braced for the fact that you will experience pain and fatigue – it's part of what we signed up for. Accept that, come to peace with it and know it only makes the triumph that much more complete.

Sunday night, whether you ran, walked or crawled, the race will long be over – and you will be going to sleep a marathoner, fully cognizant of what you (and we) always knew you were capable of.

...And exhale...

Doesn't that feel good to say -- you will be going to sleep a marathoner.

Sometimes, we worry about things so much we forget to enjoy them. For Pete's sake – DON'T be like us!!

It is natural to be nervous – this is a BIG deal – but once that gun goes off, your body and your solid training are going to take over, the jitters disappear and you get down to business.

Go Team!

Athlete's Journey:
Art Herman's Story – Part II

Art's first event with TNT was the 2009 Nike Woman's Marathon and Half Marathon in San Francisco. He'll never forget it – for many reasons.

"When I arrived at my hotel room in San Francisco, I put my suitcase on the bed and immediately picked up my cell phone to call Linda, to tell her that I had landed safely and that I was OK. It was the first time I had traveled since she had passed away."

Feeling very alone, Art headed to the lobby and ran into some TNT friends. That's when things started to get better.

"At the Expo, they have a video tribute board where they will put up a photo and a caption you send. There are several hundred of these submitted, so I was told it could take up to three hours to see Linda's photo tribute. It took five minutes. Good Karma!"

Saturday night was the Inspiration Dinner.

"I have often heard the expression, 'It's impossible to describe, you have to experience it.' Well, the Nike version is like nothing else you have ever seen. The closest comparison I can come up with is the opening ceremonies at the Olympic Games when the athletes enter the stadium. The rest of the evening you run the gamut of emotions as you listen to the speakers. When you leave, you have no doubt that you are doing a noble thing. You are so motivated, you could run through a brick wall."

Coaches' Inbox:
Event Weekend

Ok... so I need a little coaching...

Believe it or not, I am getting a little nervous. Talk to me a little about the uncharted 6.2 miles after we get through our 20. Tell me again how hundreds of thousands of people have used this program with success, and I am just freaking out over nothing. Just the fear of the unknown I suppose...

Coach here,

Let me start by saying, you don't have a monopoly on pre-marathon jitters. I still get them, whether I'm racing it or coaching it. It's totally natural.

That said, let's talk a bit about the wonder that is the human body, more specifically your body and the fact that it's already allowed you to accomplish more than you would have, perhaps, ever thought possible.

Remember that first 2 mile run? That was tough, wasn't it? Back then, 6 was probably out of the question, right? What about 13.1? My gosh... what about 17??

I'll say it again, throughout this stretch, you have steadily accomplished what you wouldn't have thought possible a few short months ago. Race day will be no different.

Now the race, as you're sensing, does start at mile 20. So, everything you do on race day needs to be focused on that truth – **don't start too fast**, stick to your fueling & run/walk plan (even if an adrenaline-induced first 6 miles makes you feel like you don't need to), hydrate, hydrate, hydrate.

Is that last 6.2 going to be pleasant? Heck no. You are going to be tested. But, as hundreds of our athletes have done before you, you are going to trust/rely on your training and take it mile-by-mile. You're going to soak up your surroundings, roll with the punches, overcome walls, stick to your fueling plan, keep moving forward, and get it done. What's your *other option? A DNF? There is no other option. Start with that notion -- and everything else just kind of falls into line.*

Athlete's Journey:
Katie Sullivan Poppert's Story – Part IV

As the days clicked by, bringing the reality of the marathon closer and closer, the enormity of what Katie had already accomplished, and what still lie ahead, bore down on her. She still couldn't quite believe that she had been able to physically come this far. She'd spent so many years on the sidelines, staying home while everyone around her hit the slopes, jumped on bikes or played tennis. But this time, she would be the one out there, the one being supported. If nothing else, at least she'd shown her kids that 'can't' truly is a four letter word. She was as ready as she was ever going to be.

"Christy and I boarded a plane early on the Friday morning before the marathon. We flew out with most of the Team In Training team and were greeted at the gate with banners and good luck signs. The feeling of warmth and camaraderie was pretty overwhelming" she said. "All of these people were here for the same reason. All of these people had fought to build their physical endurance while struggling to raise money for LLS. Many of these people were either survivors themselves or had been forced to watch a loved one suffer."

First time visitors to San Francisco, both Katie and Christy were enthralled and excited by the city's rolling landscape – and scared to death by the thought of traversing those beautifully steep hills in just three days.

That Friday night, the significance of the race, and the mission behind it, became all the more clear as Katie and Christy attended the TNT 'VIP Fundraiser' party.

"It was very heartening to see how many people were in that room," Katie said. "People who had all raised over $7,500 for the Leukemia & Lymphoma Society from around the nation. Chris was sure I'd be in the top three, but I was thrilled to discover that people were able to raise even more than I had. Much more. In fact, the top fundraiser doubled my number, coming in at just over 30,000 dollars total! She was a woman who had lost her husband the year before and delivered their baby two months after his death."

As the complimentary cocktails and the stories continued to flow, so did the tears.

"It was great for Christy to be in this company," said Katie. "For once she didn't feel alone in her struggles, alone in her fears. Here was a room full of people who were also intimately connected to the struggle of life, and death, after a blood cancer diagnosis. And these people weren't just sharing stories. They were actively DOING something. They were raising money, and awareness for the cause. It was truly inspiring."

----- **Original Message** -----
From: Your Team In Training Coaches
Alright Team,

It's almost time to get down to business!! As you prepare to take that starting line – and that finish line – we wanted to share just a few final thoughts:

A. **Legs. Lungs. Head. Heart.**

To complete an endurance event, your legs, lungs, head and heart (physical and emotional) all have to be working in concert.

Start with the notion that quitting is not an option (barring injury) and work back from there. If/when you hit a wall, are you going to go negative? Or, are you going to double down, maintain a keen focus on getting to that next mile, be willing to adjust your plan and push ahead.

Positivity rules the day. Why tell yourself you feel crummy when you could just as easily tell yourself, "You're doing this; you are fierce; you will cross that finish line!"

B. **Soak up the Experience – and Know that You Are Not Alone**
You're going to have a lot of people cheering for you on race day. You may know some of them, most of them you won't. Feed off their energy. Give

high 5's. Shout "Go Team" to your teammates. Cherish interactions with those you know. (On that note, be sure to thank your family members REGULARLY for their support during this training stretch. They are, to be sure, true unsung heroes.)

C. **Pace, Pace, Pace!**
It's an old marathoners saying and we've witnessed it at every race we've been to: The marathon begins at mile 20. You are going to be hyped up at the starting line; you are going to be like race horses bucking to get out of the gate. Resist the urge to bolt and do not let anyone push you to go faster than you know you should be going. You may feel great for the first 6, but if you're on "E" at mile 20, it is going to be a long way to the finish. You'll get there, make no mistake, but it will be tougher than it needs to be. A nice, steady pace is the better way to go.

D. **You Are Amazing!**
You should all be convinced, by your own experience so far, that the human body is, quite simply, an amazing machine, capable of allowing you to do amazing things, things you might not have thought possible a few short months ago. Your body – legs, lungs, head and heart – will get you to your finish line. Treat it well, give it the rest and fuel it needs over these next couple of weeks and believe in its ability.

My wife shared the following quote with me before my biggest race to date – we pass it on to you with great pride: "If you are lying on the beach with 80 billion grains of sand beneath you, 700 thousand ocean waves before you, 60 million stars stretched out above you, and you're still not at all impressed, I want you to think about this: the light you see reflecting from the stars is over one million years old. WOW! But then, just before you start to feel like a mere blip in the gigantic scheme of things, please remember this: yes, you are small, but you're also irreplaceable and invaluable and miraculous. Those stars don't have anything on you."

You are marvels and it's almost time to collect your reward for a season well done!

Go Team!

The Battle against Cancer: On the Front Lines

Meet cancer fighter Susan Blumel, RN, University of Nebraska Medical Center. Susan has been taking care of lymphoma patients who participate in clinical trials at the University of Nebraska Medical Center for more than 18 years.

If patients are coming to you for a unique treatment, does that mean something more standard has not worked?
There are about 60 types of lymphoma, and they are all treated very differently. Some of them, we think, can be cured, but most are incurable. Sometimes patients come to us to compare a new treatment to what is the current best standard, and sometimes patients come to a trial because they have exhausted all of their other standard options.

Talk to me about the progress and successes you see that are the result of newer treatment plans.
You know, it's just amazing. I've heard and I believe that lymphoma and leukemia research is the Rosetta Stone of research. We have come so far in learning about the biology of the disease. By learning more about the biology of the disease, we can better tailor treatments to target that biology, the process that has gone awry in the cell.

I see many new drugs becoming approved with this work. The direction that I think we're headed is treatments that will control the disease just like a patient takes medication to control high blood pressure.

What are the toughest days that you have?
The toughest days are when my patients are having a hard time. They are having problems because of their disease; they are having side effects from the treatment. On top of that, they are just trying to get through life.

So far, I've talked about how great these new treatments are, but the reality is that they don't work for everybody. There's no one thing that works for everybody. If that were the case, I probably wouldn't have a job, which would be a great problem, right?

When it's tough for the patients, what do they draw on for support?
We also have a couple of support groups in our social work area, but the patients very often draw on their family and friends, their own personal support organizations.

Have you ever had any patients talk to you about Team In Training?
I've had a few patients who have actually participated as part of the team. I had a gal who ran the L.A. Marathon. She was a runner, and I think after her cancer diagnosis it was a "let's get back to a normal life; I'm going to make this a personal goal"-kind of thing, but there was also that aspect of supporting what she had gone through, of giving back.

What do you think you've learned from your career in battling Lymphoma?
I've learned a lot about people.

I have not had cancer, and I know I can never really feel like I'm in somebody's shoes. Having said that, I do feel like I get a sense of what they are going through. People who have cancer tend to open up and talk more openly about their spirituality, family issues and personal issues in general. I think if they see that there may be an end coming, they tend to reevaluate their life and really open up about that. So, I've learned a lot through my patients about life and that helps me to take better care of them, to anticipate their needs. We try to incorporate the care into their lives as much as we can without them having to put everything on hold. The most rewarding part is just seeing my patients being able to continue their lives in as normal a way as possible.

Eleven

ON THE COURSE

"It makes me proud as a human being to know that I am doing a good thing, an unselfish thing for my fellow man, now and for years to come." – **Art Herman, TNT athlete**

―――◆―――

"I learned so much during this process – about myself, about Team In Training, and about my faith. Most of my revelations didn't come to me until Monday morning when I was waiting for my flight home. God had been with me, every step of the way." – **Kara M. Lau, TNT athlete**

A quick jolt indicated that we had met solid ground again. My head jerked forward and I instinctively grabbed the armrest as the plane – spoilers up, reverse thruster on – quickly began to slow. We had arrived.

"Welcome to San Diego," the flight attendant chimed. "The local time is 1:42. Local temperature 86 degrees. If your cell-phone is accessible, use is now permitted, but please leave your lap-belts fastened until we've come to a complete stop at our gate."

I looked out the window – a brilliant day in sunny San Diego.

"What is your favorite part?" Richard asked as our conversation, too, came in for a landing.

"I love it all," I said sincerely as I turned from the window, "but if I had to choose, I'd say race day. The hours on their feet, the training mile after mile after mile... It's all building to that."

I continued, "Race day is something you have to experience to fully understand – that electricity and nervous anticipation in the air as runners and walkers make their way to the starting line. The charge you get when that gun goes off. That 2 percent of 'amazing' made the other 98 percent of sweat and toil all worth it."

"So, you're running each of the races?" Richard asked.

"No, coaches don't run the race course from start to finish like a participant. We start here, loop around there and navigate to make sure all of our athletes are moving forward and in a good place – physically and mentally. If they aren't, it is our job to help them get there – or to a medical tent. We typically 'swim upstream' and can expect to hear 'You're going to wrong way!' no less than 4,000 times during the course of the day. Race day coaching support is a big perk of being a TNT athlete, and it is a powerful recruiting tool, the 'I want some of that for me'-effect."

I continued, "On race day, as Kelly and I prepare to 'patrol' the course, we both say a little prayer: 'Please God, help us to be in the right place for our athletes at the right time.' Time after time, He's deposited us exactly where we needed to be."

The plane remained on the tarmac, waiting for a gate to clear. We apparently had some time – so I launched into a final story.

"I'll never forget – June 23, 2012, at the Mayor's Marathon in Anchorage, Alaska, God came through like He always does..."

I didn't know Anna before that race. She was not one of "my" athletes (even though on race day EVERY TNT athlete is "my" athlete and that Coaches' athlete, and that Coaches' athlete... We are a coaching team.)

Even so, Anna and I were strangers when we crossed paths around mile 9 on a stretch of Anchorage's rocky "tank trail." An acquaintance of hers had flagged me down and alerted me that she was heading my way. (I'd guess she forced him to go on. Sometimes, especially on race day, misery does not love company.) Sure enough, a few minutes later, I spotted her.

"How are we doing?" I asked.

"Not good," she replied, barely able to hold back the tears. She was jogging at that point; I suggested we walk.

"Let's get re-set," I said gently. "What's going on?"

She was having a rough day – and she had a long way to go. That's one helpless feeling.

Stomach issues had arisen while she was travelling from her home in Washington, D.C., days before the race. She hadn't really eaten for a couple of days.

It was obvious, based on her time so far, that she'd been moving along at a pretty good clip. She was on pace for a four hour finish. Around mile eight, the wheels fell off, and it was now equally obvious that four hours wasn't going to happen. Just finishing was going to be a task.

"I am so mad," she said, the tears breaking through her defenses. This was her second marathon; it wasn't supposed to be like this.

I put my arm around her shoulder, and we walked. It sucks when things don't click. I've been there; I know. Runner after runner passed. It didn't matter anymore. We just had to keep moving forward, maybe to a med tent, maybe not.

Here's the thing about me. I really am not a talker, nor am I a quick thinker. I'm the guy who realizes what *he should have said* hours after he didn't say it. But, in these instances, after God has directed me to the right place, the Spirit, it seems, also allows me to speak in coherent tongues. (Of course, what I perceive as eloquence in my head may be something completely different in reality ...)

"We're not going to worry about four hours anymore – and we're not going to beat ourselves up about it," I said bluntly. "We just need to change the game plan."

I continued, "I know you're disappointed, but here's the thing – you see a race that went wrong; I see an opportunity for your greatest triumph. You'll remember this forever – that day that, when the chips were down, you dug deeper than you thought you could dig and you didn't quit. You kept moving forward."

I paused for punctuation: "This is going to be your finest hour."

We kept walking. She cooled down a bit, and her stomach settled. When the time seemed right, I asked if she wanted to mix a little running back in to the routine. Walk a minute. Run a minute. Walk a minute. Run a minute. On a loop.

She was game. I started my stopwatch. Walk a minute. Run a minute. The nine mile sign passed. Walk a minute. Run a minute. The 10 mile sign passed. We talked about her job, and my family, and a cool glacier tour she'd just experienced, and what brought us to Team In Training. At one point, she saw her local TNT staff person cheering on the course. Anna veered over, gave the staffer a hug and shed a few tears – and then we pushed on. Re-focus. Walk a minute. Run a minute. Walk a minute. Run a minute. That turned into walk a minute, run 90 seconds. Walk a minute. Run 90 seconds.

Around mile 11, Anna was in a better place. I asked if it would be okay for me to chug back and check on some of our other teammates. She would be fine now, she assured me. We hugged. "Finest hour," I reminded her.

As we parted, I shouted out, "Look for me at the victory party tonight. I want to know how you finished."

Sure enough, that evening, the race but a beautiful memory, I received a tap on the shoulder. It was Anna. She had found me in the celebratory chaos, and I am so glad. We hugged again and closed the loop. She had finished in less than five hours.

As the plane began to creep toward our gate, I told Richard, "I didn't know Anna before race morning, but I will remember our race day experience forever, another snapshot in my mental TNT photo album. She, like so many TNT athletes, showed me what unbelievable strength and determination looks like – 'ordinary' people doing extraordinary things, exhibiting the type of resolve that Winston Churchill spoke of during the darkest days of World War II, one of my favorite quotes: 'Never give in,' he said. 'Never give in. Never, never, never, never – in nothing, great or small, large or petty – never give in, except to convictions of honor and good sense. Never yield to the apparently overwhelming might of the enemy.'

"We need that type of resolve to train for and run marathons; we need that type of resolve to fight cancer. Your daughter had that type of resolve. My sister had that type of resolve, so did my mother-in-law."

I continued, "That race in Alaska was absolutely gorgeous. My athletes all performed admirably – and I loved being with them. But, when I think about that race – and what really justified my being there that day – I think about Anna. Her finest hour. One minute at a time... She didn't give in."

Athlete Reflections:
"What a Journey This Has Been!"
– Scott J. McCoid, TNT athlete (from his training blog)

What a journey this has been! All the hours of training prepared us to take the starting line down in Phoenix with more than 550 other Team In Training participants from all over the country. This group, with your help and support, rose over $1,600,000 to fight blood cancers!

As for the race, it was perfect!

There were a ton of people along the route, supporting friends and family and the efforts of the 7,000 runners on the course. As I was moving through some of my toughest areas, I noticed a women standing alone on a bridge. Her homemade sign caught my eye. It read: *"I am ALIVE because of YOU! Seven years cancer free! Thank YOU!"*

It put everything back into perspective for me, and from that point on, my race just got better and better. I stopped at mile 25.5 and waited for my wife Lisa. She was so strong! She hurt from the first step, but she persevered – and we finished our first marathon, hand-in-hand. I wouldn't trade it for the world!

Thank you all so much for your support through this journey. I wanted you to know that woman wasn't just holding the sign for me and the other Team In Training runners there on Sunday. She made the sign for you too. I am just the one honored to be picked as the messenger.

◆

Athlete Reflections:
Faith, God and Rock-n-Roll
– Kara M. Lau, TNT athlete,
in her own words

Have you ever wondered how the Israelites, during their desert journey to the Promised Land, could doubt the supporting hand of God – even though all the evidence showed He was there with them the whole time?

When they were enslaved, God set them free.
When they were thirsty, God provided them with water.
When they were hungry, God rained manna from the heavens.
When they were lost, God gave them a light to follow.

Over and over, they questioned Him, and He kept showing up to reassure and encourage them. Where was their faith? Why didn't they trust God? Surely, if I was in their shoes (or sandals as the case may be), I know I would have behaved better. I wouldn't have doubted Him, right?

It turns out – I was exactly like the Israelites in the desert, only my "desert" was the San Diego Rock 'n' Roll Marathon.

My story begins in January 2012. Emails were starting to come in from Team In Training's Providence Chapter about the upcoming season, a lineup which included the Providence Marathon and Half Marathon (which I'd already run with the Team) and the San Diego Rock-n-Roll Marathon (which I'd thought about running).

I'll be honest – I ignored the first few emails, but something was gnawing at the back of my mind. When I received an email offering free registration, I took that as sign. I prayed about it, talked it over with my husband, and dove in, feeling confident that this was something God wanted me to do again.

I went to the kickoff party for the spring season and talked to the coach who'd be traveling to San Diego. Since my family could not make the trip, I felt great knowing I would be traveling with someone I'd known for eight years, ever since my first race with TNT. Everything was working out!

Then, a week later, I got the news: Because the Rhode Island team was so small, we were being shifted to TNT's virtual "FLEX" team. I would now have an online coach – and the coaches from Rhode Island would not be going to San Diego.

I would now be traveling and training alone:

- No weekend group training sessions with anyone on my team
- No talking to and receiving encouragement from my coaches – face-to-face – like I'd done in the past

I was worried. Was this really God's plan?

About two weeks after I signed on, I received my answer in stark fashion when my pastor announced that his brother was recently diagnosed with leukemia. I had a renewed confidence that I was doing the right thing – and that everything would be okay.

Fundraising was going slowly, but, again, I found myself reassured. My whole family pitched in to help at a yard sale fundraiser, donating items and their time. My sister's company, Perfect Supplements, even donated a $200 Kindle Fire for me to raffle. (I still needed about $1000 so I was only going to sell 100 tickets to improve the odds.)

Every time someone bought a raffle ticket, my mom would say, "I hope you win." One of the last people to buy a ticket was a single mom with an autistic child. He used a Kindle Fire at school. His mother wanted him to have one at home but couldn't afford it. When she left, I said, "I hope you win." She was the only one I said that to.

Turns out, she didn't win – but my aunt did. My mother called her immediately and asked if she would donate the prize to the boy with autism. She said yes. It was such a blessing. The boy's mother was so grateful – and I know God's plan was being fulfilled.

After the yard sale, I only needed about $100 to finish my fundraising. God wanted me to do this race.

But what about my training goal?

That was tough. I was on my own for the most part. My coach and teammates weren't at the long runs pushing me forward.

My longest run before leaving for San Diego was only 16 miles. I tried to do 20, but never quite made it. (I am 25 pounds heavier than I was for the other marathons, which I believe impacted my training.)

My son got sick on the Tuesday before the race, and I landed in San Diego with a head cold. I started to worry again. Why would God send me all the way to California to run a marathon while I was sick?

Race morning arrived. I woke up at 3:15 a.m., got dressed and took my medicine.

I was going to do this. God was with me.

At the starting line, I huddled with two teammates from Rhode Island and team coaches, Kim and Dan. Coach Dan wore one black compression sleeve on his right leg.

"Why just one sleeve?" another racer asked.

"Because my right leg is the only one that's sore," coach replied with a smile.

Soreness aside, I now know there was another good reason for that lone compression sleeve...

The race started smoothly enough. I met a girl in the starting corral who ran the first three miles with me. After we were separated, I made it through the next six with little problem.

Then, things started to go downhill – fast.

The bottoms of my feet started to ache. I hadn't even finished half the race, and already, I felt like I couldn't run anymore. I started walking and searching for the coaches. I remember them saying they would be around mile 10. Well, 10 came and went... then 11...

Somewhere during mile 12, I saw Coach Kim. What a sight for sore eyes (and feet). She walked with me for a while, encouraging me, keeping my mind off my discomfort. I remember telling her the first half went pretty quick. I was dreading the second half. She left me just after mile 13, and I continued on my way.

This is when the bad thoughts started creeping in. I searched everywhere for inspiration but could not find it. I really started focusing on my pain.

Around mile 18, I turned a corner and saw orange peels on the ground. The tables were gone, the volunteers nowhere to be found. All that was left were the peels. I was so slow I missed out on the oranges. That is when the tears started, my confidence completely gone.

I passed a few coaches, tried to dry my tears so no one would know I was in distress, but I couldn't hold it back anymore. Finally, a coach I didn't know put his arm around me and gave me a hug. He asked if I needed anything, other than the hug. I told him the hug was enough.

Around mile 19, I was walking very slowly, and the island was looming before me. The dreaded island I had heard so much about. I was told it really was like a desert, about 10 degrees hotter than the rest of the race and three miles of sand.

I hit mile 20 and realized I still had 6 miles to go. At the pace I was going, that was another 2 hours. How was I going to do this? I felt horrible and was searching everywhere for inspiration to get me through.

Then I saw it, off in the distance, coming towards me – that one black sock!

I felt instant relief. This green shirt wasn't just any coach, it was my coach. Dan walked with me for almost two miles. My pace improved while we talked. He told me about his family, and we discussed my faith and my concerns that God wasn't at this race. All the pain I was having, in my feet, back, and hips seemed to disappear while we walked, probably because my focus wasn't on me anymore.

Suddenly the island didn't seem so scary. Though I walked the island alone, it wasn't that bad, not nearly as bad as I feared. But, if Dan hadn't come along when he did, I don't think I would have made it.

After getting off the island, I had several coaches walk with me, including Kim again. That last mile went by quickly, and when I came to the finish line, I actually ran the last bit of the race!

I learned so much during this process: about myself, about Team in Training, and about my faith. Most of my revelations didn't come to me until Monday morning when I was waiting for my flight home. God had been with me, every step of the way.

I know now it was His plan for me to do this event with TNT, His plan for me to be on Team FLEX, His plan for my sister to donate the Kindle and for my aunt to win so she could give it to the boy with autism.

When I needed Him on the course, He was there, over and over. He was the girl who ran the first three miles with me, Coach Kim, the unknown coach who gave me the hug, and Coach Dan and his one black sock.

It wasn't 40 days in the desert; it was just six-and-a-half hours on the marathon course. But, every unexpected twist and turn that shook my confidence, God was there. I wish I had realized it sooner, had seen all of the signs, and just trusted Him.

The big lesson I learned, that I hope I take with me to all my future running events, is that physical strength is not the only important factor when running a marathon. Being mentally and spiritually ready is just as – if not more – important.

Athlete Reflections:
"I Have Never Been So Humbled."
– Carol Obenauer, TNT athlete

The MRI showed two stress fractures on Carol's pelvic bone, a devastating diagnosis less than two weeks before her debut in the San Diego Rock 'N' Roll Marathon. It was too late to back out, too late to switch her funds over to another race. She was committed – to standing on the sidelines and watching. Or was she?

"I jokingly asked the doctor if I could walk a half marathon with my cane. He said 'yes' – so I did! I think I cried most of the 13.1 miles. A few of the tears were pain, but most were humility – and being completely overwhelmed. The comments that hit the hardest – and still bring a lump to my throat – went something like this: 'Thank you! I am alive because of people like you,' or, 'This is my daughter; she is a cancer survivor. Thank you!'

"It made my pain and my cane seem so insignificant. I have never been nor will probably ever be so humbled. I was so grateful for my health and strength. I was grateful for my life!"

(Carol returned to San Diego in 2010 to run the full marathon. She completed the race in memory of her brother who died four months before race day – and in honor of Judy, an inspirational TNT honored teammate who passed away about six weeks after the race.

"I ran for both of them and carried their pictures with me," Carol said. "I was and still am so proud of both of them! I love them both!")

Athlete's Journey:
Julie Petersen's Story – Part II

3:30 a.m. July 10, 2005. The alarm blared, and for the first time, Julie began to seriously question what she had gotten herself into.

"Our bus arrived shortly after we awoke to take us to the starting area. My head was rushing as I watched the streets of New York pass by my window," Julie recalled.

Her body was in denial. Every muscle twitched from nerves. Her stomach churned. She couldn't eat; she could not wake up and yet she was about to embark on the adventure of a lifetime – the *Ford New York City Olympic Distance Triathlon*.

"The gun had gone off three times now, launching the first three waves of swimmers. It was my turn now. Taking a deep breath, I jumped into the Hudson River – what a shock it was to taste salt – and quickly grabbed a waiting rope, a life-line that kept me from being pulled downstream by the current."

The gun went off a fourth time – and Julie was off.

"I can't tell you how many times I was kicked in the mouth and face or how many times my feet kicked others. I pushed myself so hard;

I needed to get ahead of the crowd so the feeling of drowning would leave my mind. I was already exhausted, and I hadn't even completed half of the swim portion yet."

Pushing on through the Hudson, she began to smell diesel fuel – and then she could taste it.

"It was horrid. After swimming though this nastiness, I actually came out of the water with a diesel fuel mustache and beard – a sight that haunts me in all the pictures I've come to cherish from this event."

As the swim came to an end, "My mind was overwhelmed with exhaustion and fear of what lie ahead," she said. "I couldn't breathe, my legs felt like over-boiled noodles, and my wet suit fought me tooth and nail the entire time I tugged at it."

Filthy water gave way to pavement and a relatively smooth – but energy depleting – 25 mile bike ride. Now, all the stood between Julie and the finish line was a 6.2 mile run – and she knew it was going to take all she had.

"My mind was done; my body, even worse yet. Even after giving birth twice in my life – twelve and a half hours of labor the first time and fourteen hours the second – I never remembered feeling this tired. My skin began to feel dirty; the salt from my sweat was drying and leaving its residue behind. Salt was the only thing that I could taste."

Tired. Hot. Her thoughts, at this point, turned to what she could hear.

"Ringing in my ears were the sounds of well-wishers rooting for me, specifically because of the charity that I had chosen to run for – Team In Training and the Leukemia & Lymphoma Society. I really wonder to this day if I would have been able to finish the race if it had not been for the thousands of people who showed up bright and early to cheer us on. It was so incredibly inspiring. I fought back tears too many times to count."

The finish line was now in sight.

"My emotions were uncontrollable! I sobbed on the shoulders of my teammates and then feverishly looked for my husband Shane. I caught sight of him as he was running across the finish line, his purple Team

In Training jersey twisted around his waist, his face bright red and his bald head shiny with sweat."

She continued, "Less than a year after he was diagnosed with testicular cancer, my husband had completed this triathlon alongside me; only he did it as a survivor! He is why I did this! He is my honored hero!"

During the course of their training, Julie and Shane raised $9,233.17 for cancer research and patient aid.

"I will cherish this endeavor for the rest of my life!"

Athlete's Journey:
Art Herman's Story – Part III

"To say that race day was 'exciting' would be an incredible understatement," Art said.

The thousands of people in the corrals on the streets of San Francisco waiting for the starting gun. Electricity in the air. The beautiful scenery, the cheering crowds and our supportive coaches motivating us along the way. The challenging hills.

"I had set a half marathon time goal of under 2 hours," he explained. "As we entered the last few miles, I was running significantly behind where I needed to be and felt as though I was starting to run out of gas. I knew I had to mentally dig deep. Two hours or more would, to me, be a failure. It had to be under two hours."

Art started to imagine everything that his beloved wife Linda had been through: the original diagnosis, the transformation, him shaving her head, the many chemo treatments, blood transfusions, the disappointment of reviewing the scans following each treatment, the final, "I'm sorry there is nothing else we can do"-meeting with the oncologist. Still, she continued to fight with experimental treatments and radiation. Art kept her in his mind as his inspiration.

"Then it happened, I suddenly felt a second wind, and felt totally refreshed, I started to really sprint the final few miles. When I saw the finish line, I just put the pedal to the metal, and spared nothing!"

1-hour-59 minutes and 57 seconds!

"After my first season with TNT in 2009, I was asked to be a mentor and have been one ever since," Art said. "I want to continue be a part of this group and support people as I had been supported when I so badly needed it. To help them with their fundraising, encourage them with their running progress and be a positive and motivating influence for them.

"That is what a mentor does. That was what my mentor, Laurie, did for me. She made the transition as comfortable as it could possibly be; she made it work for me!

"My coaches, Cheryl and James, are world class trainers and elite runners. They have helped so many people in the many years they have been with TNT. I can't say enough about how important they are.

"TNT has become a family-type of thing for me; it has become a big part of my life. It makes me proud as a human being to know that I am doing a good thing, an unselfish thing for my fellow man, now and for years to come."

Athlete's Journey:
Katie Sullivan Poppert's Story – Part V

Katie's alarm was set for 4:15 a.m.

"But have you ever noticed how, when you just know you have to get up super early, your body automatically wakes up almost every hour, just to check the clock? Needless to say, I didn't get the recommended eight hour of solid sleep that night. Not even close," she said.

Her heart was already pounding as she dressed in her long pants, long shirt that all the kids had signed, and her purple, TNT race day penny adorned with the names of all of her honored heroes.

Gobbling down some Kashi cereal and coffee, she gave the still sleeping Christy a quick squeeze and headed down to the lobby to meet the other TNT walkers who needed the early start.

"It was 5:15 by the time we jostled our way into position," Katie said.

Katie was immediately struck by how many of her fellow walkers were wearing the purple TNT pennies. Too many to count. She was inspired by all the names and pictures people had decorated them with. Inspired and choked up. It was going to be a long day, especially since her pelvis had already begun to swell. The chilly moist air was not helping.

As the field of early starters approached Fisherman's Wharf in the dark, a group of bagpipers, standing in the cold, serenaded them with beautiful music.

"Too cool," she thought. "I could also hear the seals in the distance that we had admired just the day before – and I swear they were cheering me on as I strode past. Then, just as the sun was beginning to peek through the fog, we came upon the Golden Gate Bridge. One word. Gorgeous."

Seven miles into the race, Katie had been on her feet for just under two hours, and the hills of San Francisco were beginning to climb up out of the fog. It was at this point that Katie was passed by the lead marathoner.

"That girl was sprinting. All 85 lbs. of lean muscle. But this woman, this fierce competitor, actually took the time to bend over and pick up a glove that I had dropped and handed it to me with a 'Good Job!' as she flew past. That woman embodied what this marathon was all about. There were certainly superior athletes out there to win a medal, but the overall tone was that of camaraderie. The sea of purple TNT jerseys just kept growing, and even those who weren't there with Team In Training all knew about TNT's mission. And the 20,000 marathoners out there that day had inevitably been touched by cancer at some point in their lives."

She continued, "Christy, with 'SURVIVOR' proudly displayed on her purple penny, told me that she had many women congratulate her or pat her on the back as they ran by. My favorite survivor display was a woman who had a sign on her back with a big black arrow pointing down. The sign said, 'I kicked Cancer in the....' Awesome."

As the race progressed, the marathoners split from the half marathoners.

"The full marathon took us through a gorgeous park, lined with huge trees. It was just so green in there. And moist. It was at about this point that I realized the dreaded reality of having to make a pit stop wasn't going to let me be. I veered over to a row of port-a-potties and fumbled with my fanny pack, barely getting it off and my pants down in time. Normally, I don't sit on those nasty seats, but I didn't have much choice. My legs just gave out from under me. I wondered, briefly, if anyone could even hear me in there if I got stuck. What a way to end a marathon. Luckily, I managed to get myself upright, and forced my fingers to work enough to get my pants back up and my pack refastened."

Katie had been walking since 5:30 a.m. and was now almost four hours into the marathon. She was getting tired – and grateful: grateful for the songs on her iTunes that kept her feet moving, grateful for the high school students and hundreds of other volunteers at the aid stations, with plenty of water, Gatorade, fruit and power bars, and mostly, grateful for the support of all the TNT coaches and athletes out there.

"You can never hear "Go Team!' 'You've got this!' and 'Remember why you're here!' enough times. Or, especially 'Thank you!' from the many family members and survivors who were out there supporting us along the way. Ironically, people kept saying 'Go Christy!' or 'Go Diana!' to me since their names were written on my penny, which, instead of making me want to correct them, served to give me even more incentive to keep going."

Five hours into the marathon. Katie hurt. Period.

"The good thing was that I hurt so much from the waist down, nothing was particularly standing out. My pelvis had long ago gone numb from the pain, and I had been compensating for the swelling with my usual limp. My feet hurt. My knees hurt. My toenails hurt. Instead of warming up, it had actually gotten colder in the last hour, and now we were turning onto the strip that ran alongside the ocean, normally something I would have really enjoyed. But I was having a very hard time staying focused, much less being able to take in the scenery around me. And mentally, this part was even more difficult for me since I was passing people going the other way, towards the finish line as this was the last big loop to be made."

Around mile 23, Katie hit a wall. A huge wall that seemed to envelope her on all sides. Fighting back tears, she struggled to punch at her cell phone to reach her husband Todd.

"I had made the loop and had turned around to head back toward the finish line, but the white tents just seemed to get further and further away with every step. There were people being treated for exhaustion and injuries all around me. The back of an ambulance looked unspeakably inviting," she said.

Luckily, Todd found her.

"I could barely lift my left leg by this point, the swelling was so extreme, and my right foot was burning with the extra weight it was being forced to bear. All I asked Todd was that he didn't give me what I wanted most in the world – the option to quit."

So, they walked. Todd tried to keep her mind occupied on anything he could think of.

"Of course, I reacted by lashing out at him, telling him to not say anything at all, then asking him why he wasn't talking to me. Poor guy. Those were, by far, the longest 3.6 miles I have ever walked in my entire life."

But there it was. The finish line. She was going to make it. She was going to complete 26.2 miles.

"As I dug deep and forced myself across the finish line, I felt myself begin to float. The pain in my body had brought me to a point of physical numbness and, apparently, mental hallucination. I was being cradled in the sea, held up, gently and lovingly, by each elbow by Jeffrey Roberts from above, and being pushed from behind by all the patients who had touched my life and who were no longer of this earth. I was surprised no one else could see all the sparks of energy surrounding me.

I barely even noticed the handsome fireman who handed me my coveted 'Tiffany finisher's necklace' or the girls who wrapped me up in some sort of baked potato-style cellophane blanket. The hammering throbs of pain threatened to return but subsided for just a moment, as I saw Christy in the crowd. It was one of 'those moments', where time stands still. Here, to me, was what it meant to be close to God. To be at one with the universe. Knowing that I had done this for her, and with her, and that we had made it. Together. As we limped toward each other, I couldn't hold back the tears. Tears of relief. Tears of survival. Tears of hope. Tears of friendship. Tears of love."

Team In Training Spotlight:
"Never Judge..."
– Judy Mansisdor, a runner's story,
in her own words

You've heard the saying "Never judge a book by its cover." Well, Judy would submit to you – never judge a runner by how he or she looks. Rather, look to see the heart.

If you have mistakenly inventoried your competition at the start of a race by how they look, you will be amazed at how incorrect judgments can be. Truthfully, the first will be last and the last will be first – which is to say the middle-aged guy with the six-pack abs (meaning he regularly consumes a six-pack) will surprise you and run past the 20-something gazelle-like yoga instructor who will deep-breathe the entire race at a 14 min./mile pace. Again, the heart, and not looks, is what you must measure a marathoner by.

I should know this about judging others. I am a 5'4" "solid" female. In no way do I resemble an elite athlete, and I never will. (Yet, Judy has qualified for and run the Boston Marathon, the measure of "fast" and the grail of marathons among amateur runners.) "Fast" is relative. And speed is subjugated by other qualities in the marathon, namely heart.

Marathoning is all about heart. Do you have the heart to hang in there for 26.2 miles no matter what the day throws at you: no sleep, the stomach flu, self-doubts, too many downhills, an untied shoelace, high heat and humidity, a fall, the temptation of "only doing the half." All of these I have faced, with varying degrees of success.

Most recently, I was humbled by the Nashville Country Music Marathon. (Here, please allow me a small sidebar in the "never judge a runner" conversation: never judge a race elevation profile too quickly. At a glance, the posted Nashville course looks relatively flat after mile eight or so. It's not. At mile 13, running next to a Team In Training coach from Tennessee, I asked him when the race would flatten out.

The long pause before he answered was the most truthful part of his answer. "We took the hills out of the last five miles or so" is not a statement I will agree with, ever!)

On a race day that has a phenomenal start – I've slept well, ate well, trained well; the weather is cool with clouds but no precipitation; I've had coffee and breakfast – I am the one who spends the entire race seeking out the purple shirts to yell 'GO TEAM!' or 'Good job!' to anyone who looks like they are struggling. I do this to 1) give encouragement to others, 2) to keep my mind positive and off of my own aches and pains, and 3) because sometimes the cheer and kind words come back to you and, boy, do they make a difference!

At mile 20 of the Nashville Country Music Marathon, I found myself struggling to even give a "thumbs up" to other Team In Training Teammates. I was uncharacteristically quiet. The thoughts in my head went something like this: "Breathe, breathe, breathe, water soon, get salt, breathe, ignore the blister, breathe, it's better and more fun than cancer, breathe." My total mind was absorbed in self-preservation efforts.

Around a corner at mile 23, I heard a kindred spirit ahead cheering others as he ran. "You go girl!" "Great job!" "You're rockin' it!"

I was amazed. He had a good pace and was clicking along, while encouraging every runner who looked in his direction. For reasons that will soon be apparent, everyone looked in his direction, and I wanted to be in front of this person, not behind him. Of course, as I passed him, he encouraged me: "You go girl! You've got this thing!" I forgot to mention that all these encouragements were given in a "local" accent. As I am a Yankee, I can only describe it as being southern. Sprinkle all his encouragements with "ya'll," and you will get the point.

I thanked God for that man who could do what I wanted to do at the time but could not. He was positive; he was encouraging; he was friendly; he put smiles on peoples' faces. He was selfless.

I finished the race in 4 hours and 27 minutes. The "encourager" caught up to me in the finishers shoot, where runners are corralled through the medal station, water station and food station, in that order.

By the time I passed the food, he was standing right next to me. I tapped his arm: "Thank you," I said to him. "You really helped me out at the end of the race." He put his arm around me and said, "Oh, we're all one sugar!" in that heavy local accent.

Back to our lesson about judging: more than any other person on that course, this man encouraged me and lifted me up. Never judge a runner by how he looks. Not even if he is 6'5" tall with a 6-inch red Mohawk. Not even if he is wearing tight, black spandex short shorts. Not even if he obviously frequents a tanning salon and has a fetish for ink and earrings. Not even if he has a custom safety pin spider web design on his singlet. Not even if he has more face piercings than the race has miles, including two black, phallic spikes hanging down from his nostrils. He might have a heart that will save your race!

Someday we will all be judged by how we ran the race set before us. And at that time, we will all be judged by our hearts. If you are compelled to judge a runner, particularly a marathoner, be sure to see their heart.

The Battle against Cancer: On the Front Lines

Meet cancer fight Julie Vose, M.D., M.B.A., Chief of the Oncology/Hematology Division in the Department of Internal Medicine at University of Nebraska Medical Center, where she received all her training and has been on faculty since 1990.

In the areas of lymphoma and myeloma you deal with, what are some of the promising new therapeutic approaches or drugs that you see making an impact?
I think, just as a general statement, that many of the new drugs are not chemotherapy. They are either antibody therapy, similar to rituximab (Rituxan), or they are drugs that specifically target abnormal genetic

pathways in cells so that they are not so damaging to the normal cells. I think for all of our diseases, that is the way things are going.

Is there one new drug that stands out for lymphomas?
Probably the one that is the biggest is called ibrutinib. I think that is the one that has the most positive data right now, but there are a number of ones in clinical trials. (Marketed in the U.S. as Imbruvica, ibrutinib targets B-cell malignancies. It was approved by the FDA on November 13, 2013, for the treatment of mantle cell lymphoma.)

We hear a lot of cancer patients talk about their disease as a battle or a fight. Can you talk about how you see that manifest itself in their illnesses, in getting into remission or to cure?
In general, if patients have a positive attitude and a really good support system, I think that is the biggest thing to help them get through what they have to go through. People who don't have a good support system or are always thinking negatively, I think it definitely affects them.

Twelve

CROSSING THE FINISH LINE

"I was offered a Tiffany's running necklace sitting on a silver platter from a firefighter in a tuxedo. What better way to end a marathon?" – **Shambra L. Clifford, TNT athlete**

"We had a wonderful celebratory dinner after the race. As I went to leave, I started to tear up again as I said good-bye to my coaches and to the wonderful staff members of TNT. They had been a second family to me for six months. I can say TNT is now in my blood, I am a lifer and will be doing another event!" – **Samantha Cody, TNT athlete**

I shook hands with Richard after we walked off the plane, before we went our separate ways.

"It was nice meeting you," I said. "I normally don't talk that much, but I do love talking about Team In Training. Thanks for listening."

"I really enjoyed our discussion," he said, "learning more about Team In Training and the good work you all do. You all have made quite an impact, an amazing gift you're giving to the world."

"I'm sorry for your loss," I said. "I'll be thinking of Cheryl as I work the course on Sunday."

"Thank you," he said. "Best of luck to you."

"Maybe I'll see you on the course someday," I said.

"Maybe," he chuckled. "Maybe."

One more handshake.

"God bless you," I said.

Moments later, as I walked outside the terminal, I immediately felt the sun, the breeze and the warmth on my face. Inside my carry-on: my running shoes, shorts, Coaches' jersey. Another race ahead. Millions more raised. Another step closer to someday.

----- **Original Message** -----

From: Your Team In Training Coaches

Hey you Marathoners & Half Marathoners,

We couldn't be prouder of the way you all performed and persevered out there on the course.

We know the heat was a challenge, and the aches and pains were significant in some cases, but you kept moving forward. That's grit. That's determination. That's all heart. Simply put, you shined for your honored patients, your teammates and yourselves.

Cherish the feeling. Cherish the memories and the knowledge that you now walk among the elite – a designation earned <u>not</u> by your considerable athletic prowess, but, more importantly, by your selflessness and true sacrifice. From start to finish, you've given of your very selves that others may no longer have to suffer. That earns you a place on the pedestal -- no doubt about it. May God bless you for that.

We could say that we expect nothing from you in return when we coach, but that would be a lie. The truth is we expect a rush when you cross that finish line safely and we expect to be part of a life-changing experience. You gave us that and so much more! Thank you Team!

As coaches – not to get too sentimental here – this is both a very rewarding, yet very sad time for us. We are truly going to miss our time together. Know that even though we are not "in training," we will continue to pray for your happiness and success in everything that you do.

That said, we certainly hope this is not the end of our TNT adventure together, that the glow of your accomplishment will (eventually) inspire you to undertake new physical and philanthropic challenges.

Alright Team, you are amazing people who collectively did an amazing thing. Relax, reward yourself richly, and remember – once you're part of the team, you're always part of the team.

God bless you all – and again, a truly remarkable effort out there!!

Athlete Reflections:
A TNT Member for Life
– Mackenzie Raber, TNT athlete,
in her own words

There are no words to describe those team members who were closest to me on my way to the San Diego Marathon, namely my *Sole Sisters* and TNT coaches.

Embarking on this journey was something that two of my best friends and I did together in hopes that we would hold each other accountable and support one another. We had become closer friends than ever before after five months of good and bad runs; hip, knee, and feet injuries; flop and successful fundraising efforts; and an amazing event weekend in San Diego.

The blood, sweat, tears, calluses, blisters, carbohydrates, water, and Cytomax brought us all together in a way that none of us had predicted. I could not have done it without my *Sole Sisters*.

My TNT coaches also ended up being more amazing people that I could have ever hoped to help me along my journey – from reassuring us that we could do it at the very first info meeting, to encouraging me to finish strong at mile 20 on race day, and with countless emails in between. Without our coaches and the TNT support, the essence of our team would not have been the same, and I am confident that my personal race and TNT experience would not have been as life-changing as it was without them either.

Through Team in Training, I now have a new and improved definition of a team. A team is a group of people working towards a common goal. While coming from various backgrounds and with different motivators, strengths, and weaknesses, each individual team member implicitly provides support and encouragement to the others simply with their presence.

Coaches lead by experience and example while providing a foundation of hope and inspiration to focus the efforts of the team for optimal performance, whether it be physical, emotional, or spiritual.

While I, personally, was a finisher in the 2011 San Diego Marathon, it was my team, my *Sole Sisters*, and my coaches that not only enabled my success, but gave me the motivation I needed to accomplish my goal. Team In Training will always have a special place in my heart for showing me a piece of myself that I never knew existed, cultivated only by the encouragement and support of a team. And, like any good team recruits its players, I plan to be a TNT member for life.

Coaches' Inbox:
Crossing the Finish Line

Teammates,

I can honestly say I have never experienced such a feeling of awe as I did yesterday. I cannot tell you how many times tears were brought to my eyes seeing everyone that was out there giving it their all to help people they've never met. We were a part of something much bigger out there yesterday. The camaraderie cannot be described. Runners cheering each other on. The crowds cheering for people they didn't even know. All I can say is thank you for everything and for believing in us when we may not have believed in ourselves. I cannot wait to sign up for next year and do it again! Go Team!!

Dear Coaches,

Because I don't have any children and I'm not married, I have to say that the weekend in San Francisco was the greatest weekend of my life. And such a turning point for me because now when I encounter challenges, I will say to myself, "Of course I can prevail and get through this, after all, I did just run a marathon."

I didn't know that I would be stronger mentally after all the training – what a nice unexpected gift...

Athlete's Journey:
Katie Sullivan Poppert's Story – Part VI

FINAL UPDATE: I CROSSED THE FINISH LINE!

Hello! Yes, it's true, I actually conquered 26.2 miles of hills and fog along San Francisco's beautiful coastline.

It is very difficult for me to sum up our weekend, so I'll have to use numbers to help me out:

10 minutes: The amount of time between deaths of children and adults suffering from a blood cancer in this country

$15,575.00: The grand total you all helped me achieve to ensure that the above number drastically decreases in the future

20,000: The amount of participants in the Nike Women's Marathon

6,000: The number of people from across the nation in the marathon who were involved in Team In Training

18 million (!!): The dollar amount raised by the above people for the Leukemia & Lymphoma Society for this one event

4:15 am: The hour I was up to get to the start of the race by 5:30 a.m.

50: The average temp during the marathon (Oh yeah, and there was some fog and wind too.)

25: The number of times I fought back tears along the way as I was overwhelmed by the sea of purple TNT jerseys, each with names and pictures of cancer victims

4: The number of Ghirardelli chocolate squares I snagged during the 'chocolate mile', mile 22.

500: The amount of 'good husband points' achieved by Todd when he found me at mile 23 and talked me to the finish line.

6 hrs. 35 minutes: The amount of time it took me to walk 26.2 miles

1: The number of Tiffany necklaces handed out to each finisher by a tuxedoed SF firefighter

0: The number of times I've since taken off that necklace

Too much to count: The amount of gratitude I feel to each and every one of you for helping make this physical and emotional journey possible.

THANK YOU.

The marathon was... amazing. People keep asking me about it, and that's the best word I can come up with to describe it. I thought I'd have more words to describe a 6 hour experience, but I don't. It was simply amazing. The moment of crossing the finish line was one of the best moments of my life. I still remember it vividly. I think about it constantly. It's the new memory that I pull out when the going gets tough. – Meghan Fitzpatrick, TNT athlete (from her training blog)

Coaches' Inbox:
Crossing the Finish Line

Hi Team!

I have to jump on the monkey pile and give you all a huge congratulations!! Each season I mentor I can never imagine that there will be

another with such extraordinary individuals, and each season I'm always impressed!! Nothing is out of reach for any of you!

Thank you - thank you - thank you!

Hi all,

Many wonderful words are shared, and I agree with all of the sentiments. THANKS TO THE COACHES & TNT & LLS & EVERY SINGLE PERSON IN THE TEAM! EVERYONE WAS SO AWESOME THAT I CAN'T EVEN EXPRESS IT WITH WORDS!

What drew me to the event was a feeling of helplessness against cancer that started seven years ago when I lost my father – not to a blood cancer but an evil pancreatic cancer.

I hated the feeling of not being able to do anything – and that feeling stayed with me.

Twice when running yesterday, a big sob came out of me, which surprised me. I would have never thought I could cry while running (we are supposed to be getting some happy-feel hormones, aren't we?). The thought I had was – if this weird abuse I am putting my body through could help somebody and his/her family get some relief, some help, get the necessary funds to a genius scientist to find a better solution that is really worth all the pain. It really, really is.

Big hugs to everyone. Thank you for transforming me. And congratulations to all of you!!! You are truly amazing.

Athlete Reflections:
Acting on a Dream
— Ann Herzinger, TNT athlete
in her own words

I've learned to listen when the universe gives me a dream, and today, I am a marathoner because of it.

I joined the Team in 2007, five months after losing my husband to a surprise and whirlwind illness. (If I could survive that, I knew I could survive anything.) Amazingly, at the end of that summer, I completed my first half marathon in a "blazing" 4.25 hours. (Not bad considering I use to train all summer for the 5K's I would do in the fall.)

I went on to complete two more half marathons with TNT and two on my own – and then my real story began. Again, that "something" gave me a nudge and I signed up for the Nike Women's Full Marathon in San Francisco! The thought of being surrounded by thousands of women was very empowering and spoke to my soul.

What got me through those tough miles, when it seemed like everything was a hill, was the coaches and the survivors cheering me on. Especially the survivors. They were the amazing ones.

I now wear my Tiffany finisher's necklace almost every day and remind myself that 'I DID IT!" I don't question those dreams the Universe puts in front of me anymore. I have my sights on a triathlon and a century bike ride by my 60th birthday. That's in two years. I am also reminded by that necklace that many other people are running an even tougher race to survival. I am honored to be of service to them.

Coaches' Inbox:
Crossing the Finish Line

Team,

I have been reading these emails for the past few days, and each and every one has touched my heart in ways I never expected. This whole experience and the entire team of athletes and coaches and mentors has been more than I ever thought it could be.

I was as much a beginner as I could be in the whole running/walking in a race thing, but I am addicted now. You guys have me believing I can do anything. I was inspired every week at the group trainings. You were all so encouraging to me when I was not sure I could go 5 miles, much less complete the half. You knew what to do when there were aches and pains. You knew what look to give us when we didn't want to do 10 and punk out on the 5. Your stories and experiences of the past races kept me going and believing.

Your enthusiasm is infectious. You all bring a smile to my face (Who-hoo!). You all make me proud and inspire me. Thank you so much. I might even feel the pull to get my silly self out to Zorinsky at way too early in the morning one Saturday to learn how to run the next one – because there will be another in my future!

Love to you all!

Team,

Crossing the finish line was the most incredible experience of my life. (I haven't been married and I don't have kids – I just have finish lines.) I was walking around the finishing area when a guy walked by and said to me, "Thank you. I'm a leukemia survivor." That, right there, made me forget all the agony of the last five and a half hours. It reminded me why I signed on for this in the first place. I didn't do it for myself. I did it because there was something bigger than me that was drawing me into it. I had a chance to run and be the vehicle for an organization that represents people who can't run the race for themselves. The last 20 weeks have changed my life.

Thank you to everyone who was a part of this!

Coaches,

Talk about a "do anything attitude" – I started the process already, signing up for Clarkson College. Physical Therapy! Thanks guys!

Athlete Reflections:
"Team In Training Is a Celebration."
— Angie Crawford, TNT athlete

The way Angie sees it, Team In Training is a celebration: A celebration of life, health, friends, and most of all, a celebration of each event that teaches us more about ourselves – and how to celebrate life!

Angie joined the Team in St. Louis, MO, in 2001. She had always run short distances, but never thought of doing a marathon. Now, 11 years later, she thinks, "Why not do a marathon? Or an Ironman? Or an ultra-distance run?"

"Team In Training changed my life and the lives of many people around me," she said.

While running that first race with Team – the Rock-n-Roll Marathon in San Diego – she fell in love with the city and ended up moving there in 2002 (just before running her second Rock-n-Roll Marathon as a TNT mentor). Her boyfriend saw her cross the finish line that year and decided he wanted to complete a marathon as well (a big surprise considering the disdain he held for the 1.5 miles the Navy made him run twice a year).

"That's when we ended up really falling in love with not only each other, but the idea of running together and making it a lifelong hobby," Angie said.

In 2003, Angie and Dustin crossed the Rock-n-Roll finish line holding hands, along with three other TNTers who are still their close friends. The movement spread as all of them continued to participate in events and fundraise for LLS.

"Our friends and family would have the checks made out even before we asked because they were such great supporters! Together, we have helped to raise over $30,000 for the Leukemia & Lymphoma Society," she said.

A year after Angie and Dustin were married in 2004, they moved to Jacksonville, FL. First on their to-do list was finding the local Team In Training chapter.

"In 2007, my grandmother was diagnosed with non-Hodgkin lymphoma, so we continued our fundraising," Angie said. "I am proud to say that I've done three Ironmans now, and we have done countless shorter triathlons, marathons and half marathons. But, what I am most proud of is that our parents have also joined the craziness by completing half marathons and living healthy lifestyles! We continue to motivate and inspire others – and that is truly what the TEAM is all about."

Coaches' Inbox:
Crossing the Finish Line

TNT Family,

I've been trying to think of the perfect way to say thank you for all you have done for me, but I've come to the conclusion that words can't express how much gratitude I'm feeling for this whole Team In Training experience. When I heard about TNT on the radio one morning before work, I thought, "That's it. That's just what I need." If only I knew how right I was...

The marathon has shown me that I can do anything I put my mind to and has armed me with the tools to keep fighting for my aunt Sandy and for everyone else who can't.

I'll wrap this up by saying, simply, THANK YOU for everything.

Hi coaches,

Race day was an emotional day for MANY reasons, but mostly because I came to the realization that my time with TNT was done (for now). But after some thought and reflection – I have realized that my time with TNT is far from over.

I cannot THANK YOU ENOUGH for all you have done for me. Hope to see you in the very near future.

----- **Original Message** -----
From: Your Team In Training Coaches

Hey Team,

One more from us and then we'll "sign off"...

We hope you all are getting settled back in, and we hope that post-race glow lasts a long, long time.

Unfortunately, there is a potential reality that we endurance athletes have to deal with. There may come a point when some of you might start to feel a bit blue, the post-race blues, they call it.

You've poured yourselves into this tremendous endeavor for 20 weeks – 20 weeks of structured training, group training on Saturdays, the flood of e-mails. It's been a real commitment, a real lifestyle change and now that this chapter is over, you might feel a little unsettled.

We've been there and we've found that one solution is to have something else on the horizon. It can be another run/walk with the goal of shaving a few minutes off your time. It can be a bike ride or a triathlon – with the team (hopefully) or without.

It doesn't have to be anything physical at all. One of our mentors put it best – that hopefully this experience has granted you "a newfound 'I can do anything' attitude." Maybe you want to study karate or learn to cook or finish that book that's been gathering dust on your hard-drive for the past three years...

You've done something extraordinary. Now what?

That's up to you to decide. Have fun doing it.

Never forget -- you are always welcome, if you need your "Team fix," to knock a few out with us on Saturday mornings. You know where we'll be. Otherwise, we just wanted to, again, say thank you, Team. From the bottom of our hearts, thank you.

Team In Training Spotlight:
The Genesis of TNT
– The Cleland Story – Part II

Bruce Cleland's daughter, Georgia, – the inspiration behind Team In Training and a TNT alum herself – is now in her 30's, living cancer-free. Unfortunately, the chemotherapy and radiation therapy protocols that were used in 1986 were harsh and much more aggressive than those used today. Consequently, the same treatment that saved Georgia's life also took a toll.

Early on, the Clelands were told Georgia would need cranial radiation therapy, a very serious procedure, especially for such a young person. Georgia did not escape unscathed. She suffered some brain damage and has had learning disabilities ever since. Her short-term memory skills and physical coordination skills are poor. She also has many collateral issues, including hormone imbalances which caused physical growth and development problems. Georgia experienced puberty at the age of 8 and stopped growing at about 4'6." A regimen of human growth hormone has since helped her grow to 5'3."

In 1993, after the Clelands moved to Maryland to begin a new business opportunity, they couldn't find a school in Baltimore that was suitable to Georgia's circumstances – so they helped start a school for children with special learning needs. Called the Odyssey School, Izzi Cleland was one of the founding trustees who worked so hard to make it happen. The school has been successful beyond anyone's wildest dreams, and it has since moved to a new campus which accommodates 140 children with various learning problems.

"Sometimes these things are not entirely altruistic because we respond in an effort to ease our own pain. So while on one level we're doing it for ourselves, we also have the comfort of knowing what we are doing has considerable benefit for others," said Bruce Cleland, TNT founder.

He continued, "Team in Training will always be a special part of my life, but by early 1989, I was exhausted. Our family had been completely immersed in leukemia for three years, and over that period, there was hardly a conversation in our house that didn't begin or end with the word 'leukemia' or 'TNT.' While our involvement helped us get through some very dark moments, we realized that we had responsibilities to our other children as well – and they needed more of us than we were giving them. Initially, Izzi and I considered simply reducing our involvement, but we soon realized that we were so involved that there could be no half-way. This was something we had to let go of completely. Most importantly, we realized that getting the word 'leukemia' out of our family's lexicon was in fact going to be a very important part of Georgia's healing."

Eight years later, in March 1997, a colleague named Arden Travers asked Bruce if he would sponsor her for a fundraising event she was considering doing. He was busy at the time, so he asked her to leave the brochure on his desk. When he finally got to it, he realized the brochure was describing a TNT event in which participants would compete in the 86 mile Athens-to-Atlanta ("A2A") in-line skating race in Georgia, which was to take place in October that year.

The next morning, he told Arden that he would happily sponsor her for the A2A event, but only if she would let him do it with her!

"She laughed and asked me if I was serious, and I told her that I was completely serious and later that week, I bought my first pair of in-line skates. We trained so hard for that first skating event – early every morning, long skates through the hills of rural Maryland on both weekend days. It was very hard, but we came to enjoy the camaraderie as we built a team of around 30 skaters. Over the next eight years we completed six A2A events and two 100-mile cycling events (on skates), and raised a lot of money for leukemia research! But that's another story..."

Thirteen

Someday

"The TNT experience has increased our family's self-confidence, determination and awareness of all those families in need." – **Scott & Lisa McCoid, TNT athletes**

"I have said before – and will continue to say – the endurance races I put myself through, although trying and difficult, do not hold a candle to the test of endurance and strength our honored patients go through every day while fighting cancer. When will I stop these races and end my journey with LLS? When we all cross that ultimate finish line and we find a CURE." – **Andi Mucklow, TNT athlete**

The frosted grass crunches beneath my feet. My pace quickens as I draw closer, a single tear tracking down my face. A tear of joy – and sadness.

I kneel down to speak with her, my right knee settling in the manicured grass, my finger tracing the path of the engraved marble: Sharon McCann Bearden – Sept. 3, 1966 - Feb. 6, 2005. 38 years old. Survived by her husband and two daughters.

"We did it, sis," I say.

The fugitive, that seemingly perfect villain – merciless, nimble, non-discriminatory – has met its match. Finally. That the world, in unison, is celebrating. Finally.

"All of those athletes. All of those races. All of that money raised. We did it."

And with that, my composure disappears – and I contain the tears no more.

"We cured cancer."

To learn more about Team In Training, please visit www.teamintraining.org.

Made in the USA
Charleston, SC
14 March 2015